ACHIEVING SOCIAL, EMOTIONAL, AND
COGNITIVE LEARNING IN EVERY CLASSROOM
THROUGH ACADEMIC TEAMING

THE
POWER
OF STUDENT
TEAMS

MICHAEL D. TOTH AND DAVID A. SOUSA

1400 Centrepark Blvd, Suite 1000
West Palm Beach, FL 33401
717-845-6300

email: pub@learningsciences.com
learningsciences.com / academicteaming.com

21 20 19 18 17   1 2 3 4 5 6

Publisher's Cataloging-in-Publication Data
provided by Five Rainbows Cataloging Services

Names: Toth, Michael D., author. | Sousa, David A., author.
Title: The power of student teams : achieving social, emotional, and cognitive learning in every classroom through academic teaming / Michael Toth, David Sousa.
Description: West Palm Beach, FL : Learning Sciences, 2019.
Identifiers: ISBN 978-1-943920-65-5 (paperback)
Subjects: LCSH: Team learning approach in education. | Student-centered learning. | Classroom management. | Education--Research. | Teaching--Methodology. | Learning strategies. | BISAC: EDUCATION / Teaching Methods & Materials / General. | EDUCATION / Classroom Management. | EDUCATION / Learning Styles. | EDUCATION / Professional Development.
Classification: LCC LB1025.3 .T68 2019 (print) | LCC LB1025.3 (ebook) | DDC 371.39'--dc23.

TABLE OF CONTENTS

Chapter 2

Chapter 3

Conclusion

Appendices

FOREWORDS

THE REVOLUTION UNFOLDING IN AMERICAN EDUCATION
RICK STIGGINS AUTHOR AND EDUCATIONAL CONSULTANT

A startling revolution is unfolding in American education. Students are becoming key players in their own learning rather than merely being the targets of the teaching. Michael Toth and David Sousa explain the difference herein. This change in the student's role in promoting truly effective schools is critical for two reasons: (1) we are experiencing a fundamental redefinition of the social mission of the institution we call school and that new vision needs students to be active players, and (2) the change in role allows us to take advantage of two decades of productive research on how to maximize student learning success.

This redevelopment of the social mission of schools has been precipitated by the stunningly rapid evolution of our technology, ethnic diversity, and economic inequality. These emerging realities necessitate that we rethink the skills students need to prosper in the midst of rapid cultural change. Historically, one primary school mission was to begin the process of sorting citizens into the various levels of our social and economic system. Instruction flowed out into classrooms impacting some students productively while leaving others unaffected. This effect has been acceptable given the assigned mission. Some students were supposed to succeed and occupy places high in the rank order and some were supposed to give up in hopelessness and either drop out or occupy places low in the rank order. The more spread schools could induce in achievement among students the more dependable the rank order of achievement would be by the end of high school.

However, over the past two decades of accelerating cultural change, we have realized that students who give up along the way fail to develop what we now see as essential lifelong learner proficiencies, and so are unable to survive in, let alone contribute to, our evolving social and economic system. In response, community and school leaders have decided that schools must "leave no child behind"; that is, at some level, "every student must succeed" at least in mastering lifelong learner proficiencies, leaving "each student ready for college or workplace training." If this success-oriented mission is to be fulfilled, we can no longer have any student giving up in hopelessness. Rather, the emotional dynamics of hope for some and hopelessness for many that underpinned an outdated vision of effective schools described in the previous paragraph must be replaced by practices that result in every student believing that learning success is within reach. Only then will they continue to strive for it. The social role of our schools is changing from one of sorting students into their destined roles to one of empowering students to own, take control of, and assume responsibility for their destinies.

This will require redefinition of the meaning of truly effective instruction. It can no longer be something merely broadcast into classrooms in the hope that it will impact student learning according to a normal distribution. In this book, Michael Toth and David Sousa offer a revolutionary, research-based, and very practical vision of instruction that places students in the center of teaching and learning in a joint management role with their teachers. This is a vision consistent with the new mission. Imagine, students who take responsibility for and can manage their own learning success day-to-day in the classroom. These were not the schools most of us grew up in. Toth and Sousa frame them as our attainable future.

The foundation of their vision is the idea that, in school, those who do the thinking do the learning. They rely on a strong teacher/student partnership to transfer the thinking during the learning to the student in ways that promote a strong sense of academic self-efficacy in all students, giving rise to universal motivation, engagement, and academic success. These must be the emotional dynamics of the new school mission.

I am a kindred spirit with these authors in that my life's work has centered on the promotion of the idea of student involvement in the classroom assessment process as they are learning. Two decades of research conducted around the world have led us to understand that we can engage students in an ongoing self-assessment process in ways that allow them to watch themselves grow. This, in turn, leads them to the inference that success is the direct result of their own hard work and that, therefore, they are in control of their own academic well-being. When this becomes the student's frame of reference, profound achievement gains result. Besides, and in a larger sense, if we don't define "lifelong learner" in those terms, I don't know how to define it.

But our work in classroom assessment centers only on one small facet of the larger intervention we call instruction. Toth and Sousa expand the idea of the student as a key player in the promotion of their own success to the entire instructional enterprise. Their vision represents a complete instructional model. They bring into play key attributes of learning targets, group interaction, self-monitoring, feedback, and the emotional dynamics of promoting universal student success. They share evidence of practical applications and positive impact.

There is a revolution unfolding in American education and key facets of its meaning are framed herein by Toth and Sousa. Please read on.

What if Students Were Engineers of Their Own Learning?

Carol Ann Tomlinson, Ed.D. WILLIAM CLAY PARRISH JR. PROFESSOR AND CHAIR OF
EDUCATIONAL LEADERSHIP, FOUNDATIONS, AND POLICY, UNIVERSITY OF VIRGINIA

The school where I taught for 20 years, and where I figured out what it meant to be a teacher, was rural, underfunded, and unsophisticated when I began teaching there. And it was, in a significant number of classrooms, a dynamic place for adolescents to learn. More experienced colleagues who mentored my development as a teacher insisted on our answering four questions as we made instructional plans: Why are we asking these students to work with these learning targets? What are the learning targets—how do we best express them? What will ensure student investment in the learning targets? Looking back to that time through my university-shaped lens, we were seeking student engagement with and understanding of meaning-rich content. Teachers often helped students construct the background and skills necessary to set personal learning goals, work collaboratively in a variety of instructional groupings, explore targeted content in some depth and breadth, and develop meaningful products directed at significant audiences. The school was not Nirvana. The teachers didn't walk on water. The students were just a pretty good cross section of kids across the U.S. But it was a energizing place to teach and learn.

About the time I left the public school classroom and began my second life and my work at the University of Virginia, a seismic shift was beginning in schools across the country. In an effort to raise student achievement, political decisions and subsequent mandates shifted teacher attention to preparing students to "succeed" on standardized tests. Over a relatively brief period of time, prescribed curriculum became "information" teachers must "cover" in a time span far too constricted for the amount of content that "might be on the test." Pacing guides—often more aptly thought of as "pacing mandates"—replaced an array of resources that once informed teaching and learning. With virtually no discussion of what students might best learn to help them develop as individuals and citizens of an uncertain world, teachers were conscripted to be rapid-fire dispensers of information that did little to help students understand the disciplines, themselves, or the world around them. To use Jay McTighe's analogy, teachers began having students practice for their annual physical exam rather than helping them live healthy lives.

After nearly 25 years in that mode, we have little to boast in the way of rising test scores. We do have a plethora of disengaged students who have come to see learning as a "fill-in-the-circle" process, and teachers who are exhausted from similar boredom and from pressure to winnow success from the unworkable.

What if we now found that we had the will to place students and student development on center-stage in our classrooms again? What if those classrooms were designed to foster social, emotional, and cognitive growth in all students who come our way? What if teachers were no longer dispensers of knowledge, but rather catalysts for student-owned and student-guided learning? What if students ceased being passive receptacles of conveyed information and instead learned, in collaboration with peers, to be engineers of their own learning? There is much that's attractive in that scenario, both in terms of professionalizing teaching and in terms of enlivening learning.

Still, embarking on a change of such scope is not a tweaking of the status quo in most schools, but rather is a radical change in course. We would invite almost certain disillusionment and ultimately abandonment of student-focused teaching and learning if we approached the change as though we were plucking a random jacket off a rack of possibilities and proceeding ahead. We've too often embraced the "next new thing" without a well-developed sense of its true intent, scope, or ramifications. The outcomes have nearly always been predictably sad. At a time in our history when our schools and the people in them need renewal and rejuvenation, it would be particularly costly to squander the opportunity to extend the prospects of students and teachers alike.

This book is an important contribution to the capacity of educators to construct a path forward which is considerably more promising than the one we've travelled for nearly a quarter century now. The book proposes a well-conceived model for developing student-focused instruction. It explores research from both psychology and neuroscience that contributed to the model's design. It provides careful and clear steps and stages for adopting and implementing the model. It draws insight from schools that are already implementing the model, and perhaps most importantly, the book provides both visual and written images from those schools and classrooms that help educators create images of what effectively student-focused classrooms might look like.

I appreciate the care and clarity with which Michael Toth and David Sousa have crafted, grounded, tested, explained, and illustrated the Academic Teaming model. I am grateful to be an early student of their work.

ACKNOWLEDGMENTS

We would like to thank the following reviewers:

Carol Ann Tomlinson
Author and Educational Consultant; William Clay Parrish, Jr. Professor, University of Virginia

Robin Fogarty and Brian Pete
Authors and Educational Consultants

Mariale Hardiman
Professor, Johns Hopkins School of Education

Tawana Grover
Superintendent: Grand Island Public Schools, Nebraska

Ken O'Connor
Author and Educational Consultant

Martha Kaufeldt
Author and Educational Consultant

Susan Jordan
Principal: Pinecrest Elementary, Collier County Public Schools, Florida

Patricia Saelens
Superintendent: Caroline County Public Schools, Maryland

Robin Dehlinger
Elementary Executive Director: Seminole County Public Schools, Florida

Debra Pace
Superintendent: The School District of Osceola County, Florida

Rick Stiggins
Author and Educational Consultant

Steven Tozer
Professor Emeritus of Educational Policy Studies, University of Illinois at Chicago

Toni Palmer, Amy Mancini-Marshall, and Sheree Stockwell
District and school leaders: Grand Island Public Schools, Nebraska

Elizabeth Boyle
Teacher: Walnut Middle, Grand Island Public Schools, Nebraska

Darline Karbowski
Principal: Acreage Pines Elementary, The School District of Palm Beach County, Florida

Erica Eganhouse
Instructional Coach: Howe Elementary, Des Moines Public Schools, Iowa

Jenifer Kramer
Instructional Coach/Unreleased Dean of Students: Howe Elementary, Des Moines Public Schools, Iowa

Ana Lucia Nethercote
Teacher: Acreage Pines Elementary, The School District of Palm Beach County, Florida

Emily Fazenbaker
Teacher: Preston Elementary, Caroline County Public Schools, Maryland

WE WOULD ALSO LIKE TO THANK THE STUDENTS, TEACHERS, SCHOOL
LEADERS, AND DISTRICT LEADERS AT THE FOLLOWING DISTRICTS:

Des Moines Public Schools
Des Moines, Iowa

Grand Island Public Schools
Grand Island, Nebraska

Caroline County Public Schools
Denton, Maryland

Pinellas County Schools
Largo, Florida

The Evansville Vanderburgh School Corporation
Evansville, Indiana

The School District of Palm Beach County
West Palm Beach, Florida

This book would not be possible without the dedication and committment to excellence of every LSI team member—with especial gratitude to the contributions of Taylor Barahona and Gail Shepherd.

INTRODUCTION:
THE POWER OF STUDENT-LED ACADEMIC TEAMING

Many teachers today feel beleaguered by an inflated curriculum, invading technology, dwindling resources, increased accountability for boosting test scores, and declining respect for the profession. Yet, they persist. They persist because intrinsic motivation propels them to try their best every day to help their students learn.

In this book, we demonstrate how student-led academic teaming is an instructional model that helps *all* students learn and can make teachers' jobs less stressful and more fulfilling. Academic teaming as we define the practice involves students organized into small, diverse teams with clear protocols for engaging in standards-based academic work. These protocols empower students to support each other as they work toward achieving rigorous learning targets, with much less direct guidance needed from the teacher. *The brain that does the work is the brain that learns.* Engagement skyrockets as students have the opportunity to share their thinking, respectfully challenge the thinking of their peers, and deepen their learning. As students engage with their teams, they build high ownership and accountability for their own learning, gradually taking on some of the responsibilities traditionally held by the teacher. Teachers can then shift their focus to tracking student learning, preventing achievement gaps before they happen.

> *The brain that does the work is the brain that learns.*

Student-led academic teaming—when properly implemented—raises student achievement and engagement, helps improve student behavior, and contributes to a growth mindset. Academic teaming gives all students access to rigorous core instruction and effective support, increasing equity for diverse student populations. Academic teaming accelerates the learning of English language learners, students with special needs, students struggling behaviorally or academically, and students from low socio-economic backgrounds. Time and again, we have observed students who were once shy and nonparticipating blossom forth in academic teaming, becoming active participants and valuable contributors to their teams. High-ability students are challenged to articulate their reasoning and examine new ideas and various points of view within their teams. Along with their peers, they strengthen their own understanding of academic concepts and learn leadership, responsibility, and empathy. Academic teaming helps students of all demographics to embrace accountability for their own learning. We will go so far as to say that this is one reform that really does work, and we have student achievement data and educator experiences to support it.

Student-led academic teaming goes well beyond the student grouping with which most of us are familiar. Unlike a student *group*, which is teacher directed, an *academic team* is student led, functioning with little direct guidance from the teacher. Students generate new learning within their academic teams—they are not merely paired up to process information they have learned from the teacher's instruction. Academic teaming is a daily, consistent instructional model—it is not designed for occasional large projects. Academic teaming brings in key components such as high cognitive rigor and high student autonomy, elements that are missing from other grouping methods. Rigor means having an academic culture in the classroom in which there are high expectations for all students to achieve challenging core curriculum standards—content and skills—through engagement and higher-order thinking with autonomy from the teacher.

> *Rigor means having an academic culture in the classroom in which there are high expectations for all students to achieve challenging core curriculum standards— content and skills— through engagement and higher-order thinking with autonomy from the teacher.*

STUDENT-LED ACADEMIC TEAMING: FROM SEL TO SECL

Student-led academic teaming encompasses all the social (**S**), emotional (**E**), and cognitive (**C**) components for successful learning (**L**). Thus, we have adopted the initialism **SECL** to reflect the academic teaming model's outcomes. Many programs and initiatives are focused on advancing social and emotional learning (SEL)—see the sidebars for examples of SEL competencies from the Collaborative for Academic, Social, and Emotional Learning (CASEL) and Harvard. We believe that for these social and emotional competencies to truly manifest, SEL must be embedded in an instructional model that includes rigorous cognitive learning.

In academic teams, students develop SEL competencies such as prosocial skills, self-management, and conflict resolution through working together on rigorous standards-based tasks. For example, students experience social bonding and effectively develop empathy and care in their teams because the level of cognitive rigor in the task necessitates that they rely on each other to achieve their learning targets—in other words, academic teaming creates a classroom environment where students *must* develop SEL competencies. Contrast this scenario with how SEL might be taught in a traditional classroom environment: students would receive direct instruction on empathy and care from the teacher, individually read a story illustrating empathy and care, and then write an essay about empathy and care, without actually having to practice and demonstrate these competencies with their peers.

SEL competencies should not be separate from the pursuit of cognitive rigor and academic standards. Combining social, emotional, and cognitive learning into a single integrated effort through academic teaming will ensure that our efforts to develop SEL reach their full potential in raising widescale academic achievement without being a separate program.

THE CASEL INITIATIVE

The Collaborative for Academic, Social, and Emotional Learning (CASEL) is spearheading a nationwide movement to make evidence-based social and emotional learning (SEL) an integral part of schools' curriculums from preschool through high school. This initiative supports helping students develop five SEL competencies. In brief, they include the following:

- *Self-awareness.* The ability to accurately recognize one's own emotions, thoughts, and values and how they influence one's behavior; to accurately assess one's strengths and limitations; and to develop a sound sense of confidence based on a growth mindset.

- *Social awareness.* The ability to empathize with people from diverse backgrounds and cultures and to understand social and ethical norms for behavior.

- *Responsible decision making.* The ability to make positive choices about one's personal behavior and social interactions based on ethical criteria, safety concerns, and social standards.

- *Self-management.* The ability to successfully regulate one's behaviors, thoughts, and emotions in various situations; to effectively control impulses, manage stress, and motivate oneself; and to establish and work toward personal and academic goals.

- *Relationship skills.* The ability to establish and maintain healthy and satisfying relationships with diverse individuals and groups; to cooperate with others; to listen well, communicate clearly, resist inappropriate social pressure, negotiate conflict constructively; and to seek and offer help when needed. (CASEL, 2017)

For detailed information on how student-led academic teaming aligns with CASEL's SEL Competencies, see Appendix A.

THE HARVARD SEL INITIATIVE

In 2017, the Wallace Foundation sponsored a research study conducted by Harvard University to determine the links between social and emotional learning and cognitive skills (Jones et al., 2017). The researchers suggested 12 social and emotional skills (see Table I.1) were directly related to cognitive and interpersonal skill development. In our view, student-led academic teaming, when properly implemented, promotes the development of *all* these skills.

TABLE I.1. Harvard University SEL skills. For detailed information on how student-led academic teaming aligns with the Harvard SEL initiative, see the Crosswalk for Harvard SEL Skills and Academic Teaming in Appendix B.

Cognitive Skills	• Attention control • Working memory and planning skills • Inhibitory control • Cognitive flexibility
Emotional Skills	• Emotion knowledge and expression • Emotion and behavior regulation • Empathy and perspective-taking
Interpersonal Skills	• Understanding social cues • Conflict resolution and social problem solving • Prosocial skills
Additional Skills	• Character • Mindset

Source: Jones et al. (2017).

THE URGENT NEED TO BUILD SOCIAL, EMOTIONAL, AND COGNITIVE SKILLS

Rest assured that SECL is not just a fad that will fade away in a year or so. Too many major business executives, policy makers, educators, and parents are sounding the alarm that schools are just not moving fast enough to shift away from the century-old industrial model of K–12 education, which does not promote crucial 21st-century skills. We must embrace a meaningful transformation of the teaching and learning process. We are wasting too much time overemphasizing high-stakes testing rather than helping students develop the skills they will need to be successful once they leave school.

We are faced with the challenge of preparing our students for an uncertain future. Many of the careers they will eventually pursue do not yet exist. As a consequence, we do not know what specific knowledge they will need beyond the essentials. The most recent reform initiatives in education are giving more attention to development of skills that students will need to succeed in the 21st century, rather than to just knowledge acquisition. Through the academic teaming model, students not only learn academic content, but they also interact socially and emotionally, building both advanced cognitive skills and strong interpersonal "soft" skills that will help them compete and be successful in the 21st-century workforce.

Collaboration, communication, and critical thinking are listed as priority skills by national and global organizations such as the Partnership for 21st Century Skills, Harvard Graduate School of Education, International Society for Technology in Education (ISTE), the World Economic Forum, and others. See the sidebar for 21st-century skills identified by the World Economic Forum and Appendix C for an extended list of priority 21st-century skills from different organizations.

How can students be expected to learn how to collaborate, communicate, and think critically unless they work with their peers on a daily basis and engage in rigorous, real-world, standards-based tasks? What we need is a practical and effective instructional model within which students experience academic rigor in a social-emotional context, building these 21st-century skills.

TABLE I.2. The World Economic Forum's 21st-century priority skills. Note that they encompass social, emotional, and cognitive competencies. See Appendix C for the extended list.

21st-Century Skills

- Collaboration
- Communication
- Critical thinking/problem solving
- Creativity
- Initiative
- Persistence/grit
- Adaptability
- Curiosity
- Leadership
- Social and cultural awareness

Source: World Economic Forum (2015).

Note on Effect Size: Throughout this book, you will find references to *effect size*. Generally used in meta-analyses, this is a statistical measurement that quantifies the size of the effect that an intervention has on an experimental group as compared to a control group. It is calculated as follows:

$$\text{Effect Size 5} \frac{\text{[Mean of experimental group] 2 [Mean of control group]}}{\text{Standard deviation}}$$

In educational research, effect sizes of 0.1 to 0.3 are small, 0.4 to 0.6 are medium, and 0.71 are large. The symbol for effect size is *d*.

SEL RESEARCH FINDINGS ARE PROMISING

Studies on social and emotional learning show its enormous potential. A recent meta-analysis of 82 international studies involved more than 97,000 students from kindergarten to high school, where the effects of social-emotional learning were assessed six months to 18 years after the programs ended (Taylor, Oberle, Durlak, & Weissberg, 2017). The findings showed that 3.5 years after the last intervention the academic performance of students exposed to SEL programs was an average 13 percentile points higher than their non-SEL peers. The researchers also found that behavioral problems, emotional distress, and drug use were all significantly lower for students who participated in SEL programs, while the development of social and emotional skills and positive attitudes toward one's self, others, and their school was higher.

Other studies of SEL also showed promising results regarding improved social behavior and student achievement. For instance, a study of 531 third- through fifth-grade students in urban classrooms involved in SEL interventions showed a significant reduction in aggressive behavior over the course of the school year (Portnow, Downer, & Brown, 2018). A meta-analysis of more than 135,000 students in grades pre-K to 12 found that those with SEL interventions scored significantly better in tests of mathematics, reading, and science than their non-SEL peers (Corcoran, Cheung, Kim, & Xie, 2018). Hattie's meta-analyses found a medium positive effect size of *d* 5 0.40 on student achievement for programs that enhance social skills (Hattie, 2015). This is further evidence that demonstrates how social and emotional learning promotes cognitive learning.

Research studies that link social skills development in high school with future educational achievement and earnings are very few. One impressive 10-year longitudinal study of high school students found that social skills were "as important and perhaps more important than cognitive abilities (measured by achievement tests), in predicting individual educational and occupational success" (Lleras, 2008, p. 899). Students who were considered to socialize better with their peers ended up attaining higher earnings even after controlling for cognitive abilities, family socio-economic background, and educational attainment (Lleras, 2008, p. 900). Social skills clearly matter a lot, and schools may be the only place where some students have the opportunity to learn and consistently practice social skills—student-led academic teaming can effectively aid this endeavor.

ENTER EDUCATIONAL NEUROSCIENCE

Students' social and emotional skill development is a key concern in educational neuroscience research. Educational neuroscience is an exciting new area of scientific inquiry that combines research from neuroscience, cognitive psychology, and pedagogy to determine ways of translating what we are discovering about how the brain learns into educational practice. The findings from educational neuroscience have already told us a great deal about how the brain attends, learns, and remembers, as well as what teaching strategies are more likely to be compatible with these recent discoveries.

For example, researchers note that the increasing amount of time that K–12 students are spending with their personal digital devices is having a negative effect on their social skills (Sousa, 2016). Students are spending much less of that essential face-to-face time when adults and peers teach them appropriate social behavior. Technology has transformed their social relationships from person-centered to device-centered experiences. As a consequence, they are not learning important nonverbal cues from face-to-face conversations: how to read body language, emotional expressions, facial changes, and eye contact. Young people are also becoming accustomed to using very little, if any, discretion in their digital communication—the Internet can provide anonymity, and text messaging distances the sender from having to see the pain in someone's eyes when he or she receives a hurtful message. As digital devices proliferate, this problem cuts across all socio-economic groups. Academic teaming—where students have discussions face-to-face, practice their social skills daily, and must learn to empathize with and rely on each other as they pursue rigorous standards-based tasks—offers a solution to these growing issues. We will examine further neuroscience research in Chapter 3.

A NEW PEDAGOGICAL MODEL FOR REFORM

With the pressing need to improve students' social, emotional, and cognitive skills, teachers, principals, and central office personnel are working harder than ever but still seeing too few gains for their efforts. The field of education is strewn with the corpses of well-meaning programs that never really succeeded because we were not sure of why or if they worked and because we provided little long-term support. They eventually died of neglect. Now, high-stakes testing, revised curriculum standards, and teacher accountability initiatives are all serving to divide our attention and resources so that we lose focus on the critical teaching-learning process, which is what really drives student achievement in the classroom.

A recent poll from the Education Week Research Center of more than 500 kindergarten to grade 12 teachers revealed their growing weariness with new initiatives (Loewus, 2018). Fifty-eight percent of the responding teachers replied that they had endured "way too much" or "too much" change in the past two years. Only 39 percent said they thought the new reforms had a "very positive" or "generally positive" effect on instruction. Not surprising, the respondents' main concern was the short life span of reforms. An astonishing 84 percent agreed that as soon as they get a handle on the reforms, the reforms change. One alarming result was that 44 percent said they are increasingly considering leaving the profession because of all these changes. What irony! Our attempts at improving teaching may be driving out the very people we rely on to do it.

There is a bright side to this survey. Fifty-eight percent of teachers reported that education reform has helped them improve their practice so that students learn better. That same percentage felt that the goals of the reform were in line with their goals as a teacher. These two results would imply that most teachers are willing to implement a new reform if it is compatible with their goals and if it boosts student achievement.

Instead of another reform that is simply an overlay of new content or teaching methods onto traditional instruction, we need to entirely transform our pedagogical model. Academic teaming is the one reform that has the power to attain the social, emotional, and cognitive learning outcomes that other initiatives have aspired to but did not usually accomplish. This is because academic teaming does not just change *what* students learn—it is a fundamental change in *how* students learn and how teachers teach. Learning becomes a joint responsibility between students and the teacher, creating a more effective learning environment and a more enjoyable classroom culture. Raising academic achievement becomes a shared goal. Teachers and administrators are less likely to burn out and become exhausted once students begin to shoulder some of the responsibility for learning outcomes—and, as we will detail later in this book through educator's experiences, teaching becomes more gratifying.

HOW THIS BOOK CAN HELP

Many books that propose a new instructional initiative are essentially "how-to" books. They focus mainly on helping the reader identify the strategies and materials needed to implement the proposal, and they are usually tied to the existing model of teacher-centered instruction. However, in this book, we propose a significant transition from the prevailing teacher-centered instructional model to a student-led learning environment. This major shift requires that we fully explain our rationale for the model and provide reliable evidence that it can improve student achievement. This, then, is essentially a "why" book. Why make the important move to a more brain-friendly instructional format? Because findings from brain studies reaffirm that active engagement of the learner in a teaching learning episode is more likely to result in successful learning and long-term retention of that learning. This is after all the main reason for schooling. Of course, we do make practical suggestions regarding how to implement the model over time and where one can find appropriate resources, but such implementation is successful only if the "why we should do it" is compelling and understood by those undertaking the change.

Here are some of the questions this book will answer:

- ❖ What is student-led academic teaming?
- ❖ What are the essential components of high-functioning academic teams?
- ❖ How much work and time will this take, and what is in it for me?
- ❖ How does academic teaming allow teachers to work smarter, not harder, and still get greater student achievement?
- ❖ How is academic teaming different from cooperative learning that has been around for decades?
- ❖ How does academic teaming improve social, emotional, and cognitive learning?
- ❖ How does academic teaming promote equity and access in the classroom?
- ❖ How does academic teaming develop 21st-century skills?
- ❖ How does academic teaming personalize learning?
- ❖ Does academic teaming work for diverse student populations and in challenging classroom or school environments?
- ❖ How does neuroscience support academic teaming as a brain-compatible strategy?

❖ What evidence exists to show that academic teaming improves student learning?

❖ How do school and district leaders create a vision around academic teaming and lead this instructional transformation?

We are aware that there are current books on collaborative teaming, interactive teaming, and cooperative learning—student-led academic teaming is none of these. As far as we know, there is no other book on the market that specifically addresses how to incorporate neuroscientific research into designing and implementing student teams that focus on building the strong cognitive skills and social-emotional competencies (SECL) that current instructional models lack.

CHAPTER CONTENTS

Chapter 1: Introduction to Student-Led Academic Teaming

Chapter 2: Implementing High-Functioning Academic Teams

Chapter 3: Neuroscience and Other Research Support for Academic Teaming

Chapter 4: Student-Led Academic Teaming Results

Chapter 5: Leading Classroom Change to Academic Teaming

Conclusion: Academic Teaming—Model Instruction for the 21st Century

We include a glossary, **Key Terms for Academic Teaming,** below. It may be helpful to refer to these terms as they are referenced in the text. At the end of each chapter is a page called **Points to Consider.** This is a memory jogger—an area to jot down any thoughts to consider and discuss later with colleagues and students. We also include several **Appendices** with further resources that may be helpful in understanding and communicating the connections between academic teaming and other initiatives such as Social-Emotional Learning, Equity and Access, and Growth Mindset. Further videos, case studies, and supplementary materials are available on the companion website to this book, www.AcademicTeaming.com.

WHO SHOULD USE THIS BOOK?

Classroom teachers will find this book useful because it offers a research-based and teacher-tested initiative for raising student achievement—the goal of every teacher. A basic tenet of educational neuroscience is that the brain doing the work is the brain that learns. As a consequence, in student-led academic teaming, the workload in the teaching–learning process shifts more to the students. As a result, teachers' jobs can become more joyful and less stressful.

School leaders, instructional coaches, and teacher leaders who are always looking for ways to advance student learning will find academic teaming extremely promising. The student achievement data we have collected from classrooms that implement student-led academic teaming is detailed in Chapter 4. Shifting to academic teaming also enhances the principal's important role as the building's instructional leader.

College and university instructors in preservice teacher preparation courses should also find merit in the research and suggestions we present here, both to include in their own teaching and to share with their students to better prepare them for effective instruction.

Educational policy makers will find the scientific rationale and data presented here adequate evidence that academic teaming is worthy of investigation and implementation. Too often, teachers and principals are reluctant to try out new initiatives because of concerns that policy makers on local and state school boards and in legislatures will not support their efforts. We believe the rationale for academic teaming that we present in this book, along with evidence of its success, should convince policy makers that they can confidently encourage and support this initiative.

GLOSSARY: KEY TERMS FOR ACADEMIC TEAMING

Academic team: Teams consist of two to five students working toward a common academic goal, with clear protocols for engaging in standards-based academic work. Teams are interdependent, relying on each other with *minimal* teacher guidance. Team members are accountable for each other's learning and the team culture. Teams share a vision and values in a collaborative culture that fosters trust and empowerment. The learning of the team is based on collective strengths.

Aligned task: Task that requires students to think and produce evidence of their learning at both the target's intent and taxonomy level.

Core instruction: Research-based instruction aligned to standards, designed to meet the needs of students, and delivered to all students in the class. It is the foundation of how students are expected to learn. Core instruction creates an academic culture in the classrooms with defined roles and expectations of the teacher and students, along with specific routines to support the type of core instruction.

Group: A group is a number of students who use defined roles and norms to collaborate and interact together about the content while working toward a learning target. Groups rely on the teacher for guidance and direction and are less dependent on each other. The success of the group is based on individual strengths. Individuals are accountable for their own learning. Groups can toggle between independent work and collaborative work based on the teacher's direction.

Growth mindset: The belief that personal characteristics and abilities can be learned, developed, or cultivated. Success is dependent on hard work, grit, and determination rather than on abilities one is born with. (See Appendix D for more detailed information on how academic teaming helps cultivate growth mindset.)

Independent task: Task aligned to the intent and the complexity of the learning target(s) or standard that requires individuals to practice independently with no collaboration (working silently at their group table) to produce evidence of their learning.

Instructional routines: Routines used on a regular basis by teachers and students provide students with predictable structures to build knowledge and collaborate with their peers. These routines become nearly automatic, freeing the working memory of students and teachers to focus instead on the knowledge and skills needed to be successful rather than on the procedures for accomplishing the task.

Learning target: The academic standard, or lesson-size chunk of it, that includes the knowledge and skills students will be expected to demonstrate by the end of the lesson. Students use learning targets as goals to drive their learning in every lesson.

Micro-interventions: Brief supports, such as feedback, adaptation, reteaching, and so forth, provided during a live lesson to assist an individual or group of learners struggling to attain the lesson's learning target(s) before the lesson ends.

Positive interdependence: Students in a team share common goals and perceive that working together is individually and collectively beneficial and that the team's success depends on the participation and success of all the members.

Productive struggle: Students grapple with and solve a question or problem that is just beyond their current level of understanding and that requires them to examine multiple avenues of thought. Students wrestle with ideas yet persevere and come up with solutions themselves. This struggle, while challenging and requiring deep thinking, is not frustrating. Productive struggle leads to long-term benefits like intrinsic motivation, persistence, and critical reasoning, with students more able to apply their learning to different types of problem situations.

Real-world task: Challenging task with application to real-life scenarios, involving the outside world, workplace, current events, social causes, or futuristic scenarios requiring examination and revision of knowledge, decision making, problem solving, and other complex skills. Students take on the perspective of a professional or expert role in order to meet the goals of the task, engaging in deep reasoning as student scientists, historians, poets, authors, mathematicians, artists, and musicians.

Rigor: Academic rigor does not mean hard or more content. Rigor means having an academic culture in the classroom in which there are high expectations for all students to achieve challenging core curriculum standards— content and skills—through engagement and higher-order thinking with autonomy from the teacher.

Rigorous/challenging team task: Task aligned to the intent and the complexity of the learning target(s) or standard(s) that requires a team to collaborate to produce evidence of their learning with autonomy from the teacher. A rigorous task often has multiple ways to solve, requiring evidence of deeper reasoning from students and is challenging enough to cause productive struggle, which leads to team interdependence.

Student engagement: "The amount of attention, interest, curiosity, and positive emotional connections that students have when they are learning, whether in the classroom or on their own. . . [Students'] willingness and desire to participate in their work and take genuine pleasure in accomplishing their learning goals. Their degree of engagement often determines whether they will persist when encountering obstacles and challenges and be motivated to pursue the new learning to higher levels for deeper understanding" (Sousa, 2016, p. 17)

Student evidence: Student products that the teacher can see or hear, which demonstrate the students' progress toward the learning targets.

Success criteria: Characteristics and qualities that define mastery of the learning target. Success criteria help teachers decide if their students have achieved the learning target and are used by students to track their progress to achieving the learning target. Success criteria are not a list of directions to complete a task. They are a tool the students use to plan for and gauge their mastery of the learning target for the lesson.

Task: Tasks are often confused with activities for students. A task is specifically designed for students to produce a product or evidences that they have learned or are building toward learning the target. These evidences must be either seen or heard in order to ensure the learning target was achieved by all students.

Taxonomies of educational objectives: Hierarchical systems of classification (e.g., Bloom's, Marzano's, or Webb's) that classify learning objectives into levels of complexity and difficulty. Taxonomies provide a research-based scheme to help teachers improve their learners' thinking.

Teacher verify: Through the use of learning targets and success criteria, the teacher checks for student evidence of learning and provides any needed feedback and support as the student progresses toward the learning target. Student verify is when the students take on the verifying role themselves and are confirmed by the teacher.

Team ownership: Students take responsibility for their own and for their team members' learning through their use of success criteria and learning targets to verify their learning. This team accountability system leads to students' empowerment, self-efficacy, and self-actualization.

Team talk: Student teams express ideas, respectfully challenge each other's thinking, honor each other's opinions, and disagree without being offensive, with the purpose of advancing the learning of all members of the team.

Team task: Task aligned to the intent and the complexity of the learning target(s) or standard that requires a team to collaborate to produce evidence of their learning with autonomy from the teacher. Each student may produce the same learning product, but he or she must collaborate and agree that the learning meets the requirements of the success criteria.

Tracking: Documentation of students' progress toward achieving the standard through learning targets and success criteria. Tracking is a joint effort by the teacher and student teams.

📄 POINTS TO CONSIDER: INTRODUCTION

This page is to jot down points from the Introduction to consider later and discuss with colleagues and students.

⤳ WHAT'S COMING

Chapter 1 focuses on the process of shifting core instruction from traditional teacher-centered classrooms to student-led academic teams. We discuss the gradual release of learning responsibilities from teachers to students and the fundamental change in roles for both teachers and students. We detail the positive outcomes educators can expect to see as classrooms become more student-centered, and we examine the basic systems that need to be in place to reach these incredible student outcomes.

CHAPTER 1:

INTRODUCTION TO STUDENT-LED ACADEMIC TEAMING

The focus of academic teaming is to transform to a new model of core instruction. When we look at core instruction, we are examining the classroom instructional routines and systems that dictate how students experience their learning. These instructional routines and systems can be broadly categorized into a continuum of core instruction phases, as shown in Table 1.1, moving from **heavily teacher-centered,** to **teacher-led student groups,** and finally to **high-functioning student-led academic teams** (Toth, 2016). Instructional systems include subsystems such as standards-based lesson planning, designing rigorous learning tasks, classroom management and routines, instructional strategies, and a selection of research-based teaching strategies. As teachers move away from teacher-centered learning and toward student-centered pedagogy, they plan lessons differently, have different classroom routines, use different dominant instructional strategies, have different roles for themselves and students, and have different expectations for students. These differences culminate in a classroom environment and culture that is dramatically re-envisioned as students progress toward high-functioning teams in which they exhibit maximum ownership and responsibility for their learning.

TABLE 1.1. Continuum of core instruction

Core Instruction Continuum		
Teacher-Centered Direct Instruction (low) ◄──► (high)	*Teacher-Led Student Groups* (low) ◄──► (high)	*Student-Led Academic Teams* (low) ◄──► (high)
Dominant method is lecture with independent practice. Students may sit together but work independently on tasks. Occasional pairing or grouping may augment the heavily lecture-dependent style.	Blended teaching and grouping, with equal emphasis on direct instruction and teacher-led student groups to learn and process content.	Student-led academic teams are the major part of the lesson, with supporting direct instruction to scaffold learning and then releasing the tasks to the student teams to learn, process, analyze, and create. Teams become the engine of peer learning. Teacher takes on role of master facilitator.

It should be noted that all these models—teacher-centered direct instruction, teacher-led student groups, and student-led academic teaming— can fall on a continuum of implementation that ranges from ineffective (low) to masterful (high). As a consequence, teacher-led student groups using ineffective strategies do *not* outperform students in well-planned and effective heavily direct instruction classrooms. These transitions from one core instruction to another must be done well for students to receive the learning benefits.

THE NEUROSCIENCE OF STUDENT-CENTERED INSTRUCTION

A closer look at elementary school instruction reveals that what was thought of as group work is actually independent practice in small groups, such as centers with rotations while the teacher has one of the small groups for personalized direct instruction. Much of the instruction in secondary schools still centers around the teacher. In this format, the teacher talks, and the students listen. The classroom is quiet. Students usually work alone, although there may be some occasional grouping. The teacher chooses the lesson's topics and answers students' questions. At the end of the lesson, the teacher checks if everyone is on task and has completed the work. As a result, student thinking is limited, and the learning is shallow. Why is this approach so common? There are teachers who would gladly spend time delving more deeply into major concepts, but time is the enemy. It is the one element teachers can never recover. As a consequence, the teacher-centered classroom persists because the teacher is in full control, the lesson keeps moving, little time is spent answering questions, the topic gets "covered," and the lesson ends on time.

One does not need an advanced degree in cognitive neuroscience to understand that in a teaching-learning episode the brain doing the work is the brain that learns. Whose brain is doing most of the work in this scenario? In fact, we could even argue that one of the reasons students in this classroom are not reaching their full potential is because the teacher is working too hard!

The human brain is elegantly prewired for problem solving. That is how we survived as a dominant species on this planet. We solved a variety of difficult problems to find food, shelter, and a mate. But the lecture format in many schools has reduced the brain's need to solve problems because the teacher's brain does most of the work. We need to get the students' brains working more. One way to accomplish this scenario is by use of a strategy called *productive struggle*, which involves giving students a problem to solve that is just beyond their current level of understanding. The students grapple with the problem and come up with their own solutions. Multiple neural networks are activated, and new ones are created. This process engages students in the higher-order learning and mastery of skills and content envisioned in the College and Career Readiness Standards. It promotes motivation and persistence while working out problems.

With productive struggle, we have a classroom where the students interact with the teacher and each other. The classroom is busy and noisy. Students work in teams and talk about the new learning without constant interruption from the teacher. When questions arise, the teacher first asks the team to answer and then provides feedback, if needed. However, the teacher encourages students to answer each other's questions, using the teacher as a resource. They have some choice of the topics covered in the lesson and check their own learning with some input from the teacher. In this format, the students' brains are continually processing the lesson topics. Their interactions will trigger connections between the new learning and past learning, expanding and strengthening cognitive networks. This is when students recognize real-world applications of the new learning, when they learn the value of persistence, when they learn to collaborate rather than compete, and when they use their creativity to seek answers to "what if?" questions.

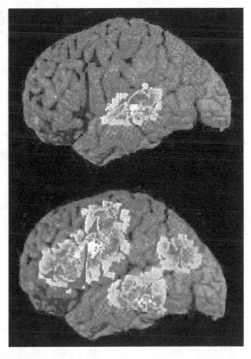

The PET scans in Figure 1.1 show the vast difference in brain activity when a person is listening to a speaker — think teacher — (top image) and when that same person is explaining what he or she is learning to someone else (bottom image). Whoever explains, learns! These images give support to the notion that the more students are engaged with their learning the greater the development of neural circuits that establish rich and consolidated cognitive networks. Just as a student can learn *about* tennis by listening to the coach explain it, that student can

FIGURE 1.1. In these PET scans of the brain's left hemisphere, the top scan shows the areas of higher activity when listening to a speaker. The lower scan shows the significantly increased activity when the brain is explaining to someone what it is learning.

only learn to *play* tennis by physically engaging with the sport. Likewise a learner's brain can only thoroughly understand and apply new learning by fully engaging with it through listening, discussing, and making mental connections to other related ideas.

Whoever explains, learns.

Productive struggle experiences are particularly valuable for younger students because their brains are working hard to construct neural networks that will help them to make sense of their world. Research studies suggest that problem solving that involves higher-order thinking provokes numerous areas of the brain to interact and connect, thereby developing robust networks that significantly increase the learner's capabilities in divergent thinking (see, e.g., Vartanian et al., 2018)

We understand that some teachers are not comfortable with this format for fear they will lose control of the lesson and that students will get off task. We also recognize that some students prefer to work alone and are reluctant to contribute to group work. We will address these concerns in detail later in the book. For now, we suggest that teachers use both formats to ensure they are meeting the needs of all students. However, our experience has been that the benefits in student-centered classrooms far outweigh the risks.

We need a simple but effective instructional model that shifts the responsibilities for the learning process from the teacher to the students. Student-led academic teaming does this.

THE THREE PHASES OF CORE INSTRUCTION

As educators walk classrooms, they are likely to recognize evidence of one of the three models of core instruction, most likely teacher-centered direct instruction or some variation of teacher-led student groups. Educators can use the tool in Table 1.2 to assess the predominant core instruction in their school or classroom.

TEACHER-CENTERED DIRECT INSTRUCTION

In a typical school, the teacher-centered direct instruction model is the most predominant. Why is this traditional model of teaching so pervasive? The teacher-centered classroom is ingrained in our thinking about how instruction in schools should look. If it is true that teachers tend to teach the way they were taught, then most teachers feel comfortable with the teacher-centered direct instruction model because that is the model most of them experienced

TABLE 1.2. The three models of core instruction (adapted from Toth, 2016, pp. 57–60). Check the evidences to determine the dominant model of core instruction students experience on a daily basis.

Teacher-Centered Direct Instruction	Teacher-Led Student Groups	DESIRED OUTCOME: Student-Led Academic Teaming
Teacher is working harder than the students. Students "compliantly" learn mostly from the teacher.	Students learn from teacher and discuss with each other.	Students are working "harder" than the teacher. Students actively learn from each other, asking difficult questions and pushing each other on the learning.
High engagement comes from the teacher personality/actions.	High engagement comes from group work.	High engagement due to the cognitive complexity of tasks and teamwork.
Teacher questions students, typically with lower-order questions and limited autonomy.	Teacher directs students, and discussions flow through the teacher with low autonomy.	Students question each other with higher-order questions and high autonomy.
Teacher's knowledge is visible. Teacher does the majority of the talking.	Student engagement is visible, and conversations around content are heard.	Student thinking and learning is visible. Student thinking and conversations dominate the lesson.
Time and energy spent on management routines.	Routines allow for productive group work.	Routines are sometimes not noticeable because students are self-motivated and self-regulate themselves and their teams.
Teacher leads.	Teacher facilitates; students participate compliantly.	Students lead and facilitate learning. Teacher provides guidance and resources.
Tasks typically only require retrieval and comprehension, such as worksheets.	Tasks typically only require retrieval and comprehension.	Tasks scaffold to analysis and utilization of knowledge.
Students sit in rows or in groups without significant interaction.	Students sit in groups or go to centers, but the tasks are not rigorous and often. Collaboration is not necessary.	Group interaction on higher-level tasks is at the center of the lesson.

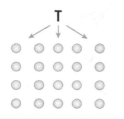

FIGURE 1.2. In the traditional teacher-centered direct instruction classroom, the teacher does most of the talking, and the students are passive listeners.

as students. Direct instruction is also efficient. Often, teachers have a packed curriculum to cover during the school year. They may see time as the enemy, and they can control the pace of coverage much more easily if direct instruction is the primary method of delivery. Nonetheless, in direct instruction, the teacher works hard to engage students in the lesson content. The flow of information is mostly one way, and the students are passive listeners and compliant learners, answering questions posed by the teacher.

The long-standing typical lesson flow in direct instruction is fundamentally sequential (see Figure 1.3). The teacher starts with a review of a previous lesson, then introduces the learning target for the day. To develop the lesson, the teacher uses various strategies to inform the students of the information and skills they should achieve in this learning episode. The students next practice the new learning under the guidance of the teacher, who provides corrective feedback as needed. Closure is the process whereby the students get one more opportunity to find sense and construct meaning from the new learning. The teacher then asks students to practice skills to meet the learning target on their own in class or as homework. Thereafter, the teacher should use some form of formative assessment to gauge how well the students have accomplished the learning target. From the results of the assessment, the teacher decides whether to reteach any parts of the lesson, provide additional examples or models, or move on.

We should make clear that we do not object to the selective use of the teacher-centered direct instruction model (illustrated in Figure 1.2). In fact, we recognize that almost any instructional approach, including teaming, requires some direct instruction. Hattie's meta-analyses reveals that direct instruction has a respectable effect size of 0.60 (Hattie, 2015).

Our concern arises when direct instruction becomes the *predominant model for all students most of the time*. Because the sequence remains essentially the same each day, students know what to expect when they cross the classroom's threshold. The forthcoming lesson lacks the unexpected, what

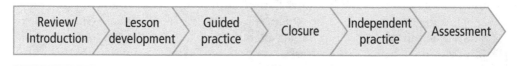

FIGURE 1.3. The diagram shows the typical sequential flow of a lesson during direct instruction.

we call *novelty*, which is the one environmental factor that really gets the brain's attention. With students spending so many hours every day on their digital devices, their brains have become accustomed to novelty, such as screen images changing every few seconds.

It is not just the lack of novelty, it is the lack of engagement of the students' brains that inevitably leads to disinterest and detachment from the lesson. Furthermore, if we consider the 21st-century priority skills mentioned in the introduction—collaboration, communication, and critical thinking—it becomes apparent that students will only successfully learn and develop these skills by *actively* participating in their learning. They need to discuss aloud with each other their understandings, determine how they can be connected to what they already know, and make predictions about how the new learning can be applied to the real world. In many instances, direct instruction does not allow this to happen.

Finally, in the teacher-centered classroom, the teacher holds control and full responsibility for student learning. As shown in Figure 1.4, when teacher effort and control is high, student ownership and autonomy is low. Students as a result are not as empowered in a teacher-centered classroom. The burden for "pushing" and "pulling" students to master more rigorous academic standards and to succeed on tougher assessments is primarily on the teacher. As classrooms continue to diversify with English language learners, students with disabilities, high-ability students, and students from lower socio-economic status, the demands on teachers continue to grow. To move students to greater learning gains in a traditional direct instruction yet diverse classroom, the teacher must work harder. With teacher fatigue, burnout, and attrition increasing, we believe there is a better way.

Relationship of Teacher Effort/Control to Student Ownership and Autonomy

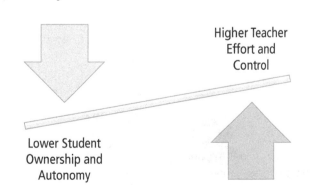

FIGURE 1.4. The relationship between teacher effort and control to student ownership and autonomy.

TEACHER-LED STUDENT GROUPS

The second model in the continuum is teacher-led student groups. In this model, teacher-led student group work balances direct instruction with roughly equal emphasis in classrooms. Researchers have been gathering evidence of the efficacy of student-centered classrooms, sometimes referred to as *learner-centered teaching* or *active learning*, for many years. Although definitions of *student-centered* vary, a 2014 Stanford case study, for example, used quantitative data to track achievement and extensive observations, surveys, and interviews to evaluate student-centered learning. In all schools, the researchers found that in student-centered classrooms, "African American, Latino, economically disadvantaged, and English learner students achieved above—and, in some cases, substantially above—similar students in their districts and in the state" who were receiving traditional instruction (Stanford Center for Opportunity Policy in Education, 2014).

Once the teacher determines that students are ready for teacher-led group learning, they will rearrange the classroom, as shown in Figure 1.5. Schools most often misidentify their instruction as predominantly student-centered, assuming that because students are in centers or sitting in furniture groups that they have *some* students working together that their classrooms are student-centered. But that is not the case. Effective student-centered classrooms go well beyond simply arranging students in groups to augment traditional teacher-centered classrooms. The authentically student-centered classroom requires more than merely having students sit and work together.

In authentically student-centered classrooms, as we define and have developed them, teachers plan lessons with group tasks aligned to academic standards. Students working together have clear roles and individual accountability as well as group accountability. There are norms for student talk and use of academic vocabulary as well as established protocols for encouraging social and emotional skill development such as conflict resolution. The teacher alternates between delivering short

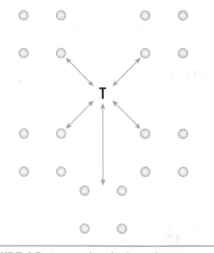

FIGURE 1.5. In teacher-led student groups, students discuss and process content, but the teacher is directing, correcting, and prompting the work.

mini-lectures, laying and scaffolding foundational concepts, and encouraging group work. This allows students to engage meaningfully with the content as they produce visible and audible evidence of their learning while they interact with their peers. Even the mini-lectures are more interactive, as students move away from raised hands to random calling or students calling on each other. Students actively build on one another's thinking as new knowledge is introduced. The teacher uses the mini-lecture to quickly set the stage for the group work to do the heavy lifting, as students dig into the content and increase their understanding. The teacher walks from group to group, ensuring students are on task and equitably sharing the workload and every student is showing *evidence* of learning for the lesson's standards-based outcomes. If students are not showing evidence of the learning target, the teacher provides micro-interventions to struggling students through feedback, encouragement, additional explanation, or pulling a group of the struggling learners for remediation and then quickly returning them to their groups to complete their task. One of the biggest benefits of providing a more equitable learning experience for all students is that the teacher has time during group work to ensure all students are learning through micro-interventions.

In these classrooms, the students work as hard as their teachers. The teacher begins to skillfully shift the heavy lifting burden to where it should be—on the students. In teacher-led student groups, teachers are no longer on stage doing most of the talking. Rather, there are expectations for respectful student dialogue. Students examine what they are learning and show teachers how they have achieved mastery of the lesson learning target(s). Some of the traditional teacher-led routines, such as gauging the degree of learning, begin to shift to the students, where students track their own learning using standards-based learning targets and success criteria.

Core instruction in teacher-led student groups engages students more thoroughly than in teacher-centered instruction because students are required to be active learners. Because every student participates in the group, less confident learners—those that typically hold back from participating by not raising their hands to answer teacher's questions—now engage with their group members in the content, creating academic safety and greater access and equity for all learners. (See Appendix E for more information about how student-led academic teaming leads to increased equity and access for all learners in the classroom). Student voice increases as students participate in discussions about what they are learning. Students' sense of belonging increases as the group culture develops. Moreover, students begin developing a greater sense of accomplishment and self-esteem as they track their learning progress on the success criteria to reach the standards-based learning target. These benefits emerge whenever the teacher demonstrates the willingness to transfer some of the responsibility for instruction to student group discussion and collaboration.

STUDENT—LED ACADEMIC TEAMING

Once the groundwork has been laid in the previous phase with teacher-led student groups, the classroom is ready to advance to the highest level of core instruction in the continuum—student-led academic teaming, as shown in Figure 1.6. For this shift to occur, the roles of teacher and students adjust again. As the group processes have matured and students have self-regulated with roles and norms during group tasks, the teacher releases even more responsibility to the groups, forming them into academic teams. Academic teaming becomes the engine of learning that dominates the lesson, with direct instruction becoming a supporting role to provide foundational content. The predominant role of the teacher transitions to master facilitator.

Now, the teacher enables students to reach higher levels of ownership and engagement. The teacher plans lessons with team tasks that are challenging and connect to the real world, encouraging students to take on professional roles as student mathematicians, poets, historians, scientists, or authors. Students' voices and choices are included as students and the teacher set joint standards-based goals for their teams and plan how the tasks connect to the real-world and to students' interests.

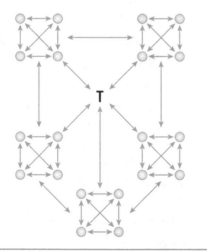

When students' choices are included in setting their challenging goals and connecting their work to the world they are experiencing, their ownership and engagement rockets to another level. As student autonomy increases, and students experience success and bond with peers, their appetite for learning grows. At the same time, the teacher establishes new norms for the teams, including the expectation of peer support and accountability, creating a student-owned accountability system within the teams. The teacher increases the challenge of the tasks to slightly beyond the current ability of the students to encourage productive struggle, creating interdependence

FIGURE 1.6. In student-led academic teaming, students drive their own and their peers' learning, holding themselves accountable for reaching their learning targets, while the teacher shifts to the role of facilitator and verifies the learning.

among the team members because they need to support and peer coach each other to attain the rigorous task. As Figure 1.6 illustrates, the hallmark of a team versus a group is the interdependence within the high-functioning team culture that allows students to self-actualize and develop empathy by supporting other members to attain the learning target. Team success becomes as important as personal success. Figure 1.6 also shows that the students are peer teaching and coaching each other. The critical point is that the students take on another responsibility of providing micro-interventions to the peers who are struggling with the content. This role in other core instruction models is reserved for the teacher, but with student-led academic teams, the students personalize the learning and peer supports for their team members. At this point in a mature academic team, the students take responsibility to ensure learning is accessible and equitable among all team members. This is where social and emotional learning thrives alongside cognitive processing.

A large body of research has documented the effects of perceived competence (Newmann, Wehlage, & Lamborn, 1992), secure connection with others (Stipek, 1996), organization around a clear purpose (Newmann et al., 1992), and meaningful and relevant work (Stipek, 1996) on increased learning engagement. In true student-led academic teams, students begin to connect what they are learning with the real-world problems they are witnessing and experiencing. This connection of academics to the real world is a significant driver for even greater engagement and more complex learning. When this team dynamic and real-world application spark ignites, it becomes the fire that turns students from passive receivers of content to passionate scholars of content. Student groups mature into high-functioning academic *teams*. Table 1.3 summarizes the shifts we have been discussing.

As students exercise their creativity in engaging in real-world tasks, they experience authentic learning. Authentic learning can be defined as follows:

> Authentic learning engages all the senses allowing students to create a meaningful, useful, shared outcome. They are real life tasks, or simulated tasks that provide the learner with opportunities to connect directly with the real world.

> Instead of vicariously discussing topics and regurgitating information in a traditional industrial age modality, authentic learning provides a learner with support to achieve a tangible, useful product worth sharing with their community and their world.

> Our greatest shortcoming in education these past few years has been to ignore the brain research that is richly available to us that affirms that implementing multi-sensory activities, pursuing meaningful tasks, exploring a variety of skills with real world applications is optimal learning and that it needs to be practiced regularly. (Revington, n.d.)

In Chapter 2, we will explore these concepts in greater detail, including how to create the classroom enabling conditions necessary for student-led academic teams to flourish.

TABLE 1.3. Roles, dynamics, and percentages of direct instruction shift as learning moves from direct instruction to student-led academic teams

Teacher-Centered Direct Instruction	Teacher-Led Student Groups	Student-Led Academic Teams
Approximate Ranges 80–100 percent Direct Instruction 0–20 percent Group Work	*Approximate Ranges* 50 percent Direct Instruction 50 percent Group Work	*Approximate Ranges* 30 percent Direct Instruction 70 percent Teamwork (Teams also engage in enough independent practice tasks to ensure fluency.)
Teacher-centered is the dominant experience of students in the classroom resulting in the academic culture of the classroom. Students roles and responsibilities are restricted to listening compliantly and quietly doing their own work, not distracting their classmates, talking when spoken to by the teacher, and so forth. This creates a climate conducive to learning by lecture.	Group-centered is the dominant experience of the students in the classroom because they are spending enough time in their teacher-led student groups to form a group learning culture that transforms the academic classroom culture toward student centered. Students have roles and responsibilities for their learning and that of their peers. The classroom becomes noisier, with students processing content in their groups and tracking their own learning. Access and equity increase as all students are engaged with the content in their groups, experiencing academic safety. Students develop prosocial skills, self-regulation, belonging, and acceptance in peer groups. This creates a climate conducive to learning in teacher-led group work.	Team-centered is the dominant experience of students in the classroom because they spend most of the lesson time learning in their teams. A team culture develops, where students peer-teach, support, debate, and reason together with challenging tasks requiring deep learning, productive struggle, and interdependence among the members to ensure everyone reaches his or her fullest potential. Students co-own each other's learning and personalize learning for each other. Students develop leadership, conflict resolution, goal setting, and executive function skills. Students develop empathy because they are responsible for the learning and support of each member of the team. This creates a climate conducive to learning in student-led academic teams.

STUDENT AND TEACHER ROLES TRANSFORMED

> "When we are in groups and we have a team with each other, we all have the mindset of finishing the work, so we work hard to do what we need to do. If our team doesn't understand what to do, we ask another team instead of asking the teacher. We're all comfortable with each other, so we collaborate together, and it's no problem."
> —*High school student, G.W. Carver High School, Muscogee, GA*

As classrooms gradually shift toward academic teaming, students assume *ownership* of the roles to work together to accomplish the group learning task with as little support from the teacher as possible. Students learn to self-regulate and work together with established norms for their groups. Challenging group tasks and peer discussions increase cognitive engagement. The teacher intentionally cultivates student ownership and self-regulation within the group roles and structures—the gateway for greater student achievement.

During this process of shifting from teacher-centered instruction, to teacher-led student groups, and finally to student-led academic teams, the roles of the teacher and students transform. This transformation is the primary indicator that core instruction is moving along the continuum. The teacher has *chosen* to share control and responsibility with the students in their group structures. This granting of defined control to student roles and norms within the group structure is critical to developing student ownership, fostering the growth and well-being critical to increased student self-regulation (Boekaerts & Corno, 2005). Multiple studies have also pointed to student engagement, autonomy, and goal-setting in learning—all attributes of student-centered instruction—as a factor in self-regulation (Karoly, 1993; Tadich, Deed, Campbell, & Prain, 2007). Or as researcher Guy Claxton has put it, student-centered instruction inculcates what he calls the "capacity to learn." Claxton challenges teachers to think about the following:

> . . . what would it mean to organize your classroom and your pedagogy in such a way that every day, little by little, in the midst of literacy hour, or during an experiment on magnets, your students were learning to learn more robustly, more broadly, more skillfully and more flexibly? They will need to design activities that deliberately focus on stretching each aspect of learning capacity and ensure that this goal is not eclipsed by a more familiar focus on the acquisition of knowledge and the completion of tasks. (Claxton, 2007, pp. 121–122)

As student ownership increases and group dynamics mature, groups gradually become more self-sufficient and able to take on greater responsibility, including increasingly complex group learning tasks. Students' experience an increased role in their own assessment for learning by tracking their individual progress toward learning targets.

Increased student autonomy and goal-focus allow the teacher to step back further, releasing more responsibility to the students. A teacher who never fully releases control to students will end up a "helicopter teacher," hovering and rescuing struggling students and thus keeping students dependent. Such dependent students are prevented from developing ownership and self-regulation through self-reliance. Gradual release of responsibility *requires* a release of control to students to help them develop responsibility. This process further helps students develop social and emotional skills during teamwork on their academic learning tasks.

Figure 1.7 illustrates the transformed roles of the teacher and the students with the academic teaming process becoming the engine of learning that also provides access and equity to all learners. The teacher's role shifts to providing absolute clarity on what is to be learned and planning for rigorous standards-aligned team learning tasks. The teacher briefly provides direct instruction mini-lessons on foundational content and skills, preserving most of the lesson time for teams to engage in the rigorous learning tasks. The team roles and norms require students to develop, use, and master social, emotional, and cognitive skills while accomplishing demanding academic learning.

Our observations at the Learning Sciences Applied Research Center support the conclusion that when student group work is restricted to simply being an augment to a traditional teacher-centered classroom, these learning

Academic Teaming Produces SECL Outcomes

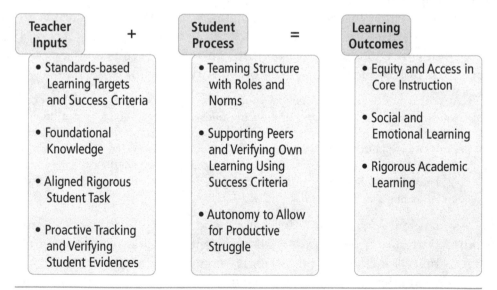

FIGURE 1.7. Academic teaming instructional model.

benefits will not materialize. *The classroom culture cannot transform unless the roles of teacher and students materially transform.* A group or team culture does not form unless such change happens. A healthy team culture resulting from roles, norms, and challenging tasks with greater autonomy from the teacher enables the student members to develop and practice social and emotional skills. They develop prosocial skills, self-management of emotions, time management and organizational skills, empathy for team members different than their own background, and leadership skills. Our research has shown that student-led academic teaming both increases student achievement and decreases negative behavior. We will discuss these findings in detail in Chapter 4.

> *Classroom culture cannot transform unless the roles of teacher and students materially transform.*

CLASSROOM FORMATIVE ASSESSMENT OR ASSESSMENT FOR LEARNING

A significant body of research supports that implementing classroom formative assessment, also called *assessment FOR learning*, in every lesson can improve student learning when implemented well (Black & Wiliam, 1998; Graham, Hebert, & Harris, 2015). Classroom assessment FOR learning does not refer to quizzes or tests but rather the minute-to-minute process of checking for evidence of learning in students' work—either auditory or visual—and making just-in-time adjustments if the evidence of learning is not suitably present as the lesson unfolds. This process of classroom assessment FOR learning should be visible and active for *both* the teacher and the students.

Student participation in assessing their own learning is grounded in research and is a critical component of comprehensive and balanced assessment systems. Susan M. Brookhart, Jay McTighe, Richard J. Stiggins, and Dylan Wiliam outline this idea in their 2019 white paper about creating assessment systems that benefit students. Research shows that when students are more active in taking responsibility for their own learning and assessment, assessment supports their learning; when students aren't active, assessment does not support their learning as well (Zimmerman & Schunk, 2011).

Academic teaming embeds classroom assessment FOR learning as an active process between the teacher and students, with both involved in the teaching-learning process. It starts with providing academic teams with clear standards-based learning targets and success criteria to define *what* they will learn and *how* they will know when they have learned it. Next, team members track their individual progress as well as their team members' progress to the learning target by noting each evidence on the success criteria when it is accomplished during the learning tasks. Students support each other with peer tutoring and peer teaching for members struggling with the learning task, but team norms prevent students from simply sharing answers. Each student must accomplish her or his own learning with peer support from the team. In a study on peer tutoring, students who engaged in peer tutoring in student-led groups learned nearly as much as students who received one-on-one tutoring from the teacher (Schacter, 2000).

While the academic teams are engaged in tasks, the teacher has the role of checking that teams accurately self-assess their achievement of the learning targets. Students may well be confident but incorrect in their learning. The teacher's role is to facilitate the classroom formative assessment process during academic teaming, to ensure teams are effective in supporting struggling learners, and to provide extra direct support, when necessary, during the lesson. The goal is for every student to demonstrate evidence of learning the target for every lesson, thereby closing the achievement gap one lesson at a time.

See Appendix F for how academic teaming aligns to the five key strategies of formative assessment, and Appendix G for how academic teaming aligns to the seven strategies of assessment FOR learning.

GETTING STARTED AND GROWING IN MASTERY

As the teacher gets started in making the shift to student-centered instruction, he or she will experiment with student groups to fine-tune new routines, roles, norms, and instructional flow. The teacher needs to observe these newly formed student groups for a healthy and productive group dynamic and ensure that students are talking about the content and engaged in the expected work utilizing their roles and group norms. The teacher learns quickly the differences between good and bad noise and is proactive at heading off group dynamic issues that will impede progress as students learn to regulate themselves and their newfound autonomy.

In short, the teacher needs to teach students how to learn *together*, which will be awkward at first, especially for older students who have become comfortable with teacher-centered instruction. Because students are expected to share the load with the teacher by organizing, self-directing, and thinking for themselves, they need the teacher's encouragement and praise as they take steps to build their confidence.

Our observations of classrooms where students and teachers use the strategies more masterfully indicate that student groups become more focused and effective. Teachers can gauge how successfully their groups are evolving by answering these questions: How much responsibility and ownership has the teacher successfully transferred to the group structures? How have the capabilities of the groups elevated in self-reliance? Have the groups become engines of learning for their members?

As the student groups transform into high-functioning academic teams, they require less intervention from their teacher in order to reach more rigorous standards-based learning targets or lesson outcomes. Students are tracking their own progress to learning targets and that of their peers, thereby building *interdependence* within the team. As teachers increase the level of rigor of the learning tasks, student discussions reach critical thinking levels with reasoning, evidence-based claims, peer coaching, revising their knowledge, and rich debates. This gradually increasing rigor results in students engaging in *productive* struggle, which is a necessary ingredient for effective and long-term learning.

"Students are having fun in their learning and owning their learning, they're out of their seats, they're questioning their peers, they're collaborating. They're engaged in rich tasks that are aligned to the standards."
—*Principal Willette Houston, Bear Creek Elementary, Pinellas County, FL*

"What surprised me this year with the students was the level of coaching they've been able to provide each other—they're mini facilitators, they're able to lead each other to the desired outcomes, and they've really taken on mini leadership roles in the classroom. The outcome is stronger because the students have a say-so in what they need to achieve."
—*Jake Van Winkle, second-grade teacher, Glenwood Leadership Academy,*
Evansville, IN

THE POWER TO CHANGE

Transforming from a teacher-centered to student-centered classroom environment is not an easy transition for many teachers. It requires coaching and training for the school leaders and faculty—and strong principal leadership to start the process. Teachers worry about losing control of their classes and wonder what their new role will entail. What might a principal think during a walkthrough? What if the class becomes too noisy or chaotic? How will they be evaluated, if they are not displaying traditional teaching skills? What are the risks to classroom culture if student-centered learning does not produce results right away? These are all valid concerns.

As we have emphasized throughout this book, we have found that, when implemented correctly, students quickly show increased evidence of ownership, self-regulation, and learning—across all school environments from 100 percent free and reduced price lunch schools to affluent ones. Once teachers and students get a taste of success, teachers become the biggest advocates for the shift to student-centered instruction. The change process often starts with principal leadership and ends with teacher leadership. We will discuss our own findings in more detail in Chapter 4, but we will offer one brief example here:

At one high school in Georgia serving 100 percent students from disadvantaged backgrounds, the school leader had committed to integrating academic teaming into all classrooms. We walked through classrooms with this principal at the end of the year. As we watched students engaging in critical thinking and respectful but passionate debates about the content they were learning in their peer groups, he told us, with tears welling up, "I *knew* our kids were smart. I *knew* they were capable of this." Indeed, all students, all classrooms, and all schools are capable of supporting authentic student-centered classrooms. When the transformation occurs in every classroom and student ownership ignites, it unlocks the *unrealized* potential of schools.

> *All students, all classrooms, and all schools are capable of supporting authentic student-centered classrooms. When the transformation occurs in every classroom, and student ownership ignites, it unlocks the unrealized potential of schools.*

COOPERATIVE LEARNING VERSUS ACADEMIC TEAMING

We are sometimes asked "What are the differences between cooperative learning and academic teaming?" There has been much written on the differences between cooperative and collaborative processes. Academic teaming is founded on a collaborative process. We classify cooperative learning under the broader category of teacher-led student groups—the middle core instruction in the continuum (Table 1.1. Continuum of core instruction). Although they share some components, academic teaming has much higher potential for student achievement from the teaming process because students are granted greater autonomy and responsibility. Cooperative learning tends to be more teacher directed and supported, with more emphasis on closed-ended tasks that are suitable for lower taxonomy levels of retrieval and comprehension. Scripted cooperative learning programs are addressed more fully at the end of Chapter 2.

QUESTIONS FOR REFLECTION

We firmly believe that teachers want all their students to reach their full potential. They recognize that there are factors that can limit this goal, such as differences in ability, language, academic preparation, and behavior. But most teachers will try any strategy that they are convinced can help them achieve their goal of *all* students learning and succeeding. The question is whether the investment of teachers' time and energy to learn about the strategy, implement it, and gauge its impact will reap significant positive benefits for their students.

Teachers considering the transitions we recommend in this book may ask themselves the following questions to reflect on the instructional shifts we have outlined here.

- ❖ What percentage of time do you devote to direct instruction and independent practice in your classes?
- ❖ What would be the benefits to you as a teacher to decrease your talking, act more like a facilitator, and allow time for more collaborative group work?
- ❖ What would be the benefits to your students?
- ❖ How will encouraging students to express their ideas, interact with peers academically, and take intellectual risks in the classroom help them navigate in the real world?
- ❖ What ideas in this chapter resonated with you and could lead to more student autonomy in your classroom?
- ❖ How comfortable are you with student learning being a little messy? Chaotic? With letting your students productively struggle?
- ❖ If you are a school leader, how will what you learned in this chapter affect your choices of professional learning for your staff?

Teachers' responses to these questions will give them a good idea about their mindset and comfort with making the transition to student-led academic teams. Throughout this book we have included stories from teachers who made the transition to classroom teaming, some of whom were initially hesitant to try it for various reasons. Even so, they made the leap, and all were enthusiastic about their results.

"I have seen a lot more productive conversations that kids are having compared to years past. There's always the kid who is very content to allow other students to do the learning, and they can kind of just sit and listen. And what I've seen is a lot more active participation on the part of *all* of the kids. Really, one of the things that has been a surprise this year is how quickly kids will move into a position to take care of a group member who is struggling or not understanding and asking questions. Even just gentle questions: 'Okay, what do you think?' and 'Well, what was your opinion on this?' It's not something we always get to see from 13- and 14-year-olds. So that's been an exciting transformation, the care and concern they have for each other as learners."

—*Elizabeth Boyle, Walnut Middle School, Grand Island, NE*

(See Appendix A for more detailed information on how academic teaming aligns to CASEL's SEL competencies, such as ethical responsibility and respect for others; see Appendix B for further alignments between teaming and SEL outcomes from the Harvard study.)

📄 POINTS TO CONSIDER: CHAPTER 1

If students were not *required* to come to your class, would they?

This page is to jot down points from Chapter 1 to consider later and discuss with colleagues and students.

_____

_____

_____

_____

_____

_____

_____

_____

_____

_____

_____

_____

_____

_____

_____

_____

_____

_____

_____

_____

_____

_____

⇗ WHAT'S COMING

Chapter 2 explains the enabling conditions and guidelines for forming high-functioning academic teams and examines how these teams work. We discuss how to support the development of academic teams, how to sustain them over time, and how to differentiate teams that are performing poorly from those that are performing well. We include observations about successful classroom teams we have witnessed and comments from teachers who are implementing high-functioning academic teams.

CHAPTER 2:

IMPLEMENTING HIGH-FUNCTIONING ACADEMIC TEAMS

The student-led academic teaming model we advocate in this book is a strategy that teachers can use effectively for daily student tasks and lessons, not just for occasional large projects. Teachers use academic teaming within traditional classroom schedules, from a 40-minute period to block scheduling. Academic teaming may be, and should be, practiced effectively for everyday learning in lesson-sized, rigorous tasks that foster students' ability to think more deeply about content and apply their knowledge to new situations in a real-world context. Also note, academic teaming should be viewed as the core instruction that can *accelerate* student achievement and development and, therefore, should not be used as a privilege that students can lose as a consequence for misbehavior or as less important time for struggling readers or English language learners to work on remedial computer programs while their peers work in teams. When academic teaming becomes the norm in classrooms, students and teachers reap the immense benefits of social, emotional, and cognitive learning to their full potential. Teaming develops the whole child and builds life and executive function skills, but certain conditions must be present for teaming to succeed.

THE ENABLING CONDITIONS

Most attempts at academic teaming falter because teachers do not set the *enabling conditions* for teaming from the outset. Not doing so means teachers will expend far more effort correcting teaming issues arising throughout the implementation process. Having the correct enabling conditions from the start will aid greatly in achieving the goal of a transition to student-led academic teams. J. Richard Hackman (2004, 2011) described these enabling conditions during a long career spent studying how effective adult teams function. The Learning Sciences Applied Research Center has adapted Hackman's research on enabling conditions, in part as the foundation of our own work with student-led academic teams to include four conditions. As shown in Figure 2.1, the team (1) is defined, (2) has roles and clear norms of conduct, (3) has a clear and compelling purpose, and (4) has a supportive environment.

Enabling Conditions

Defined Team:
- Stability
- Team size
- Diversity

Roles and Clear Norms of Conduct:
- Facilitator and checker
- Respect and accountability

Clear and Compelling Purpose:
- Productive struggle
- Accountability
- Interdependence

A Supportive Environment:
- Recognition
- Resources
- Teacher coaching

FIGURE 2.1. The four enabling conditions for high-functioning academic teams.

Once a teacher clearly sets these enabling conditions, he or she reduces the need for interventions to rescue the team. If these enabling conditions are not set up with a strong foundation, the effects of positive teaming will erode and eventually require greater investment of time to correct. Teachers can spare themselves and their students some stress and frustration by planning for academic teaming properly from the start.

Teaming requires a persistent commitment from both teachers and students. Classrooms will not be fully immersed in teaming in a day or in a week, but teachers and learners will see gradual progress and can celebrate small wins each day. Momentum will build and create a positive spiral of success if the four enabling conditions outlined above are present. Now, let us take a detailed look at each of the conditions.

A DEFINED TEAM: STABILITY, TEAM SIZE, AND DIVERSITY

STABILITY

A real team has stable membership. One of the things a novice teaming teacher should avoid is frequently switching team members because it robs the team of the "norming" students must go through to fit into their team roles and responsibilities. Teams need a measure of stability to become high functioning. Over time, team members will create the social bonds necessary for the team to accomplish rigorous, complex tasks; this bonding process instills a sense of belonging and purpose.

As Hackman (2011) emphasizes, "Conventional wisdom is wrong. Research findings overwhelmingly support the proposition that teams with stable membership have healthier dynamics and perform better than those which constantly have to deal with the arrival of new members and the departure of veterans" (p. 61). Stable teams allow members to settle in and get to the task quickly, instead of losing time in repeatedly orienting new members to the social norms of the group. Stable teams gradually develop shared commitment to the team and a sense of belonging and caring for one another; they accept each other's differences. Team effectiveness depends in part on the same set of people having enough time together to learn how to work collectively and support each other.

Classrooms with highly mobile student populations will experience the arrival and departure of team members regularly. Once the teams have formed and established team routines and norms, teachers have reported success in incorporating new team members due to serving highly mobile students or the occasional need to move team members for academic or behavioral reasons. In many classrooms, we have seen that once the team has "normed" successfully, team members themselves are fully prepared and capable of inducting the new members into the team routines and expected norms.

Enabling Conditions

Defined Team:
- Stability
- Team size
- Diversity

Roles and Clear Norms of Conduct:
- Facilitator and checker
- Respect and accountability

Clear and Compelling Purpose:
- Productive struggle
- Accountability
- Interdependence

A Supportive Environment:
- Recognition
- Resources
- Teacher coaching

FIGURE 2.2. The first enabling condition for high-functioning teams: defined team.

There is a caveat to stable team membership. Stable teams can, over time, begin to rely too much on habitual routines and plateau in their engagement. Members may stop pushing each other's thinking and learning. To avoid this, teachers should rotate the roles of the team members at reasonable intervals. That allows for team cohesion without staleness. Rotating roles offers team members the opportunity to experience both leadership and followership roles and skills. The teacher should also increase the rigor of the learning tasks at regular intervals when the teams show the capacity and supportive culture to handle the level of difficulty. This combination of sharing roles and increasing the rigor of the tasks will keep the teams vibrant and cognitively engaged.

TEAM SIZE AND DIVERSITY

Team size matters—a lot. For academic teams to become high functioning, they need to be small enough to aid in communication and collaboration but also large enough to contain a diversity of opinions, cultural backgrounds, genders, personalities, and skills. From our implementation work in over

1,000 classrooms, we have found that the ideal size is four students, but a range of two to five also works. The larger the team, the more communication links or "communication overheads" there are, which may complicate team dynamics considerably—including making it harder for all members to contribute to the work equally.

As business writer Geoffrey Keating (2016) has warned, the larger the number of members, the more complex the communication. Keating's diagrams show the complexity of attempting to collaborate with too many members. Large groups have less time for debate, meetings are harder to manage, and member participation is likely to become less equal. A meeting of eight people, as shown in Figure 2.3, results in 28 communication connections, a tangle that may impede productive work. The same is certainly true of student teams.

In a study on the influence of group size in discussions, Fay, Garrod, and Carletta (2000) put undergraduate students in groups of five and groups of 10 and asked the groups to engage in complex decision making. Their results indicated that the smaller groups were better able to "take into account the range of opinions among group members," whereas the larger groups were better suited "to disseminate a particular opinion through a dominant group member" (Fay et al., 2000, p. 485). Students benefit from considering the viewpoints of their diverse team members, rather than simply accepting the viewpoint of the most vocal member, and thus will thrive in a smaller group size with interactive dialogue.

Communications Quickly Become Complex

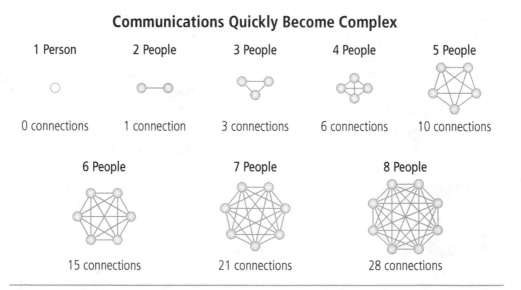

FIGURE 2.3. As groups grow in size, communication becomes increasingly more complicated (adapted from Keating, 2016).

Hackman (2011) also notes that the larger the team, the greater the opportunity for members to hide out, coast, or engage in "social loafing." Hackman explains, "Groups whose size is in the double digits are almost certain to encounter free-riding or 'social-loafing' problems. And they run the real risk of spending nearly as much time coordinating among members as actually performing the team's work" (p. 93).

In sum, keep teams as small and diverse as possible. The positive effects of team diversity have been well documented (Kearney, Gebert, & Voelpel, 2009; Roberge & van Dick, 2010; Stahl, Maznevski, Voigt, & Jonsen, 2009). Recent research has also found that mixed-gender teams in the business world are more productive (Badal, 2014; Hoogendoorn, Oosterbeek, & van Praag, 2013). Earlier studies noted the benefits of "informational diversity" as being conducive to productive teaming because it stirs "constructive conflict" (Jehn, Northcraft, & Neale, 1999). Our own observations, coupled with teachers' testimony, indicate that, time and again, academic teams have helped integrate students with special needs and English language learners into academic conversations—in many cases, students with long-term struggles have flourished well beyond expectations.

COMPOSING HETEROGENEOUS TEAMS

"My biggest challenge with implementing teaming in my fourth-grade class was having students from different academic and behavioral backgrounds working collaboratively, especially students reading two or more years below grade level. This has been resolved by strategically putting higher- and lower-level students in the same groups (heterogeneous mixing). It has also helped to have specific 'jobs' for each team role, so each student is forced to take ownership."

—*Deane Waters, fourth-grade teacher: Greensboro Elementary School, Caroline County, Maryland*

At least in the beginning, teachers should avoid letting students select their own teams. Students tend to pick their friends, and cliques and rivalries will inevitably form. Groups composed of diverse viewpoints, abilities, backgrounds, and skills tend to work best because congeniality and like-minded thinking can compromise critical thinking. Teams composed of members with similar backgrounds may fall victim to groupthink, which limits learning opportunities. We have seen examples, particularly in lower grades, of students being permitted to mix up and choose their teams toward the end of the year, once they have the norms and principles of teaming well established. But teachers should be aware of the possible pitfalls and should handle team composition with care, always ensuring diversity on every team.

One of the best gifts we can give students is to provide opportunities to develop empathy, including for those who are different from themselves. This opportunity reflects the *S* and the *E* of SECL—all students are building social and emotional skills. Groups should have a mix of English language learners, academically high-ability students, and students who are cognitively diverse. Students who may not normally socialize together will find a way to work toward a common purpose (Capodieci, Rivetti, & Cornoldi, 2016). Such adaptability and empathy are some of the critical life skills that will help students succeed in today's and tomorrow's diverse workforce.

FROM THE CLASSROOM: ORGANIZING DIVERSE TEAMS

An observer in a third-grade classroom at Starr Elementary, in Grand Island, Nebraska, shared this evidence.

Toward the end of the school year, I visited a classroom where students were working in teams of four. The students were used to working with each other by this time—debating, discussing, and following the procedures of a high-performance team. I noticed one student, Josh, who had a small behavior reminder card taped to his desk. He was sitting on a cushion, and he also had the option of using his desk as a standing desk.

When I asked the teacher about Josh, she told me he had an individualized education program (IEP) that allowed him to use different strategies to manage his ADHD as well as his emotions. I wondered if the other students would be frustrated by his accommodations, or with having to coach and support him in the work. But it turned out the opposite was true. Josh was able to participate because the other team members treated him as an equal. I watched closely as they took turns talking, and when Josh participated, they did a group high-five. I asked the teacher if she had coached the team to do this as a way to motivate them. "No," she assured me. "They came up with this strategy on their own."

At one point, Josh started having a minor meltdown because he was falling behind on recording his answers. One girl in the group said, "It's okay, Josh. Just do what you can. We are here to help you." Josh put his head down and started to cry. The teacher came over and whispered to Josh that it was okay and repeated that his team was there to help him.

"I can't keep up," Josh said. "I don't want to do it anymore." The team facilitator came up with an idea. "Why don't you just put the page number, Josh, instead of writing everything? That will save you time." The teacher nodded approval at the team facilitator, patted Josh's back, and walked away. Josh slowly picked his head up and got back on task.

The students worked as a team and didn't give up on each other. I noted that this was a group who probably wouldn't choose to work with each other under other circumstances, but their different backgrounds actually helped them learn. The team facilitator and other members learned patience, empathy, and peer support. And Josh learned to feel accepted, truly part of a team, despite his disabilities.

—*Sara Croll, Learning Sciences International Research and Development*

I wondered aloud if the other students would be frustrated by his accommodations, or with having to coach and support him in the work. But it turned out the opposite was true. Josh was able to participate because the other team members treated him as an equal.

ROLES AND CLEAR NORMS OF CONDUCT

Enabling Conditions

Defined Team:
- Stability
- Team size
- Diversity

Roles and Clear Norms of Conduct:
- **Facilitator and checker**
- **Respect and accountability**

Clear and Compelling Purpose:
- Productive struggle
- Accountability
- Interdependence

A Supportive Environment:
- Recognition
- Resources
- Teacher coaching

FIGURE 2.4. The second enabling condition for high-functioning academic teams: roles and clear norms of conduct.

ESTABLISHING TEAM NORMS FOR ACCOUNTABILITY

"I think my biggest success with academic teaming was establishing group roles—keeping the same role within their teams for the day and applying that role in every subject. Each team member has a specific role, and each role has specific jobs. My most unexpected success with academic teams was their accountable talk. I provided students with 'academic talk' bookmarks for them to keep on their desks at all times. The bookmarks have question and sentence stems on them. Then, I added even more rigorous (analytical) question stems for them to begin asking. They have blown me away with their accountable talk that they use everywhere, all the time in the classroom, and their higher-level analysis questioning."

—*Deane Waters, fourth-grade teacher: Greensboro Elementary School, Caroline County, Maryland*

Two roles are critical for a high-functioning team—team **facilitator** (one member who ensures that everyone participates equally and keeps time) and **success criteria quality checker** (one member who tracks the team's progress toward the learning target and ensures that every member is learning according to the success criteria). In addition, each student has the responsibility to track his or her own progress using the success criteria. Teachers may experiment with additional roles for the teams beyond these. In a quad team structure, two formal roles among the four team members seem to work well. Some teachers prefer to create additional roles so every team member has a role. We have seen both approaches work.

Beyond these two roles, the teacher and students will collectively compose and commit to a set of norms for teamwork. Norms clearly define which behaviors are valued inside the group and which behaviors are not valued. A high level of commitment to team norms leads to higher ownership of teamwork and a greater ability for students to regulate their own behavior. As the teams progress, their norms may evolve to support increasingly rigorous work. Norms also support student teams to autonomously plan how to tackle a task (the division of work, time keeping, record keeping, and so on, all of which are necessary real-life skills).

Norms support the full utilization of all team members' knowledge and skills. Indeed, well thought-out and collectively agreed-upon norms encourage a climate within the teams where individual members feel safe to take personal and interpersonal risks in their learning. They learn to develop both academic and interpersonal skills, to take on new roles, and to practice not only leadership but also followership—a role as important as leadership in effective teaming. Teachers should create team norms with the goal to actively help students share and help each other appropriately.

Remember that one of the goals of academic teams is for students' internal motivation to become self-sustaining within the team, as the members continue to experience small successes and gain confidence in the teaming process. Their increasing confidence creates a positive spiral, where small accomplishments and peer coaching in turn foster greater accomplishments and self-confidence in each team member and in the team as a whole. This positive spiral allows the teacher to release greater responsibility to the team and to assign more challenging tasks that the team is willing and able to rise to. The intentional and purposeful outcome of academic teaming is that students develop a sense of belonging and earned self-esteem.

Figures 2.5, 2.6, and 2.7 offer some examples of team norms. Teachers often use protocols, anchor charts, and other devices to implement roles and norms. (Visit the companion website for additional examples at www.AcademicTeaming.com.) In some cases, the teachers and students collaboratively created and agreed on the norms. The idea is to ensure that students know how to respectfully challenge each other's thinking and assumptions. Team norms are usually posted on classroom walls or on student desks so that team members can refer to them often and so that peers and teachers can gently redirect students who fail to observe the norms.

What does a good team

👀 Look like	👂 Sound like
• Working cooperatively (sharing supplies)	• On topic
• Following directions (on task)	• Respectful conversation (use kind words)
• Smiling 😊	• Be polite (please, thank you)
• Taking turns	• Good listeners

FIGURE 2.5. Example of norms for academic teams.

Our Team Is Off-Track—Now What?

Problem	Solution
A team member is gone	• Agree on someone else to do the job or take turns
Someone is not doing their share of the work	• Remind them of the equal work success criteria • Ask if they need help
A team member is messing around or off topic	• Remind them of the group/partner work success criteria • Remind them you count on them to do their part
We are stuck or confused	• Send scouts to other teams
We are arguing	• Take a 1 minute break • Give each person a turn to talk • Decide or vote together
We are done!	• Check all success criteria • Finish or fix problems • Find ways to improve • Reflect on your teamwork

FIGURE 2.6. Example of conflict resolution norms for student teams.

I can partner with anyone!

- Get started right away
- Work the whole time
- Talk on subject ... stay focused
- Do equal work
- Share all materials
- Respect other teams
- Level 1 voice
- Be respectful to each other
- Come up with ideas together

FIGURE 2.7. Students and teachers work collaboratively to develop team norms for procedures, behavior, and communication.

We often suggest the following:

1. Clear norms for what to do when team members are struggling with the learning

2. Norms to ensure equal and high effort from all members

3. Norms for team talk, which ensure that a few members do not dominate the group's thinking and that team members respectfully push on each other's thinking

As teachers create team norms in their classrooms, they may decide to create specific norms for resolving conflict.

FROM THE CLASSROOM: CREATING AND REINFORCING TEAM NORMS AND ROLES

An observer in a fourth-grade classroom at Howe Elementary, in Des Moines, Iowa, shared this story.

In a fourth-grade classroom I visited, students were working in teams of four. They had team norms, success criteria, and question stems available at their desks to help them stay on task and push each other's thinking. Their roles were also identified. The team facilitator wore a badge noting her role.

For the task they were working on that day, the students were expected to push their teammates' thinking by using textual evidence to support their answers. The team read a passage, then looked at each section of the passage to determine the text structure. The students took turns providing their answers, while their teammates asked two questions:

—How do you know?

—What is your evidence?

The team facilitator helped move the conversation along and encouraged each member to speak up. Those who disagreed adhered to the team norms, politely saying, "I disagree with you because . . ."

One of the students disagreed but could not explain to the team why. The facilitator prompted the student, asking, "Why do you disagree? What is your thinking?" At first, the student sat there without responding. Next, he replied with an off-task response. In a calm, friendly, yet assertive tone, the facilitator got him back on track, saying, "Come on, let's stay on task." When the boy still didn't answer after a few seconds, another teammate tried another strategy. "Let's look at the text in paragraph three."

"Oh, I didn't see that!" the student exclaimed. The facilitator brought the group back, asking, "So now do we all agree that the text structure is *problem and solution*?"

This teamwork took place without coaching from the teacher. She was observing other groups but never interjected with this team. It turned out the team was able to help a struggling peer, have a sophisticated conversation, and come to a conclusion on their own because the structures were in place to support clear team norms and roles.

—*Sara Croll, Learning Sciences International Research and Development*

(See Appendix A for more details on how academic teaming aligns with CASEL's SEL competencies, such as communication and impulse control.)

Enabling Conditions

Defined Team:
- Stability
- Team size
- Diversity

Roles and Clear Norms of Conduct:
- Facilitator and checker
- Respect and accountability

Clear and Compelling Purpose:
- **Productive struggle**
- **Accountability**
- **Interdependence**

A Supportive Environment:
- Recognition
- Resources
- Teacher coaching

FIGURE 2.8. The third enabling condition for high-functioning academic teams: clear and compelling purpose.

A CLEAR AND COMPELLING PURPOSE: PRODUCTIVE STRUGGLE, ACCOUNTABILITY, AND INTERDEPENDENCE

Teams will not properly form unless they have a compelling purpose. Vangrieken, Boon, Dochy, and Kyndt (2017) argue that a truly entitative team (they define *entitativity* as the level of "teamness" a team has) comes together when team members recognize they need each other. "There needs to be *a reason to collaborate* [our italics] and work in teams as opposed to loosely coupled individuals. When there is no collective task or goal to start with, and individuals can perform their tasks individually, there is no need for a highly entitative team to tackle these individualized tasks" (p. 30).

Teachers can help teams find a compelling purpose by providing challenging tasks—ideally, tasks that have some relation to the real world or to students' interests and tasks that ignite the team's passion for learning something new.

A well-designed, challenging team task has three key characteristics. It should require the following in order to achieve the task:

1. *Cognitive stretch,* resulting in productive struggle—which creates *challenge* and fosters the need for *interdependence* within the team as members draw on each other's knowledge and skills to complete the task

2. *Individual accountability* for learning

3. Evidence of learning the full *intent and rigor* of the standard(s)

Often, we have found that teachers need professional development and additional time for designing rigorous tasks for academic teams that represent the full intent and rigor of the standards. Teachers will initially invest more time in planning until they create a bank of lesson-sized rigorous tasks for their curriculum. Once they complete this bank, they will have free time to move from creating to maintaining and improving the bank of tasks. For examples of team tasks, please see www.AcademicTeaming.com.

PRODUCTIVE STRUGGLE

Based on conclusions from the Third International Mathematical and Science Study (TIMSS), Hiebert and Grouws (2007), Hiebert and Wearne (2003), and others have identified the benefits of productive struggle in fostering resilience, perseverance, engagement in learning, and achievement. Productive struggle, which has been defined as working with knowledge and skills slightly above the student's current level of competency, occurs when students are thinking their way through a difficult solution or grappling with complex issues *without* interruptions from the teacher. One teacher we spoke to called this "the beautiful struggle" as she observed how her students developed a growth mindset and gained academically through the process of grappling with complex knowledge. Students who engage in productive struggle, *even when seeming to fail,* have been shown to outperform those who do not (Kapur, 2008).

> One teacher we spoke to called this "the beautiful struggle" as she observed how her students developed a growth mindset and gained academically through the process of grappling with complex knowledge.

During productive struggle in their teams, students are in the highest state of cognitive engagement. Brain scanning studies show that learners' brains are working hard when they are engaged in solving complex problems (Dandan et al., 2013). Multiple neural networks are contributing to the effort, searching for past experiences that can help clarify and solve the problem. The students are engaging in deep debate and reasoning about the content. They are working through various solutions and pitfalls as they test ideas. The teacher must step back even more to allow students to engage in productive struggle and must resist the urge to step in. This means the teacher must intentionally grant more autonomy to the student teams to allow for productive struggle to occur while students tackle complex problems and turn to their peers for support within the team. Studies show that this arrangement frequently results in students working together to find the correct solution (Granberg, 2016). The need for interdependence arises from productive struggle as students turn to team members for support.

If teachers *over*-support, fostering dependence rather than independence, they will rob students of productive struggle and cognitive growth (Stein, Smith, Henningsen, & Silver, 2009). Rescuing students too early is an understandable impulse of many teachers, but teachers must restrain themselves to allow students to develop self-reliance. A challenging team task at a level that requires the use of higher-order thinking skills and a bit of reach for the students will require them to engage in productive struggle. On the other hand, unproductive struggle—when students are merely frustrated rather than thinking and working hard—will occur when learning has not been sufficiently scaffolded to build foundational information and skills so that students are ready to stretch for the task at hand.

TABLE 2.1. Are students struggling productively or just struggling?

Nonstruggle	Productive struggle	Unproductive struggle
Students don't have to reach for the answer.	Students must work for the answer.	The answer is too far out of reach.
Students recall and repeat answers from memory.	Students debate, revise thinking, and generate hypotheses to find answers.	Despite reasonable time and effort, students cannot come to an answer.
Resources may be consulted, but no high-level thinking is involved (simple information retrieval).	Students must engage with resources (discuss with peers, interpret readings).	Resources are insufficient, unclear, or too complex.
Students feel bored and passive.	Students feel challenged, empowered, and engaged.	Students feel frustrated and give up or disengage completely.
Student teams are nonexistent or not being utilized to their full potential.	Student teams are functioning well—confident, interdependent.	Student teams experience interpersonal conflict due to frustration or become unmotivated.

It is important to note that we are trying to break old habits, where students are dependent on teachers to clear up misconceptions. Likewise, we are helping teachers break ingrained habits of jumping in without giving students the time to solve a problem. Instead, we are building the habit of *interdependence*, which we will discuss below.

CULTIVATING PRODUCTIVE STRUGGLE

We have seen teachers masterfully creating the noisy energy and engagement of an academic game by not giving the answer to students, cultivating productive struggle. If the teacher provides the answer too quickly, then the game is over. Thinking and learning stops. During one math lesson we observed, when teams shared their work and explained their thinking, students saw they had different ways to solve a complex problem. The teams also discovered they had different answers. When the teacher asked students to figure out which answers were correct, the teams engaged in debate, applying mathematical principles in what became an extended game of mathematical thinking.

As the teams stalled in their progress, the teacher masterfully facilitated their process by tossing out a hint about a mathematical principle the class had learned earlier. The teams dug in with renewed vigor to solve the problem. In the end, students found the correct answer, but not all teams solved the problem in the same way. Each team explained its thinking to arrive at the same answers. Only then did the teacher affirm that their work was correct.

This was a fourth-grade inclusion classroom taking on pre-algebra equations. There were many aha! moments as students made connections and applied various mathematical concepts. In short, students were solving difficult math problems using mathematical thinking just as mathematicians would. If at any point the teacher had told them which answer was correct, the learning would have ceased. Instead, she raised the bar for her students, who productively struggled, with great engagement. Contrast this scene with the traditional mathematics class, where the teacher works through an example problem, followed by students doing independent practice problems, repeating the process again and again.

We are not describing student groups as most of us have known or experienced them. These are student teams working at a much higher level. These teams become a powerful engine of learning, allowing students to take on responsibility for their learning and reach greater complexity of learning tasks. At each step, students are developing a sense of belonging with their peers in their academic groups. As they track and see their progress in reaching group and individual goals, they build earned self-esteem and internalize the idea that they are smart and capable. Each step builds upon another as students begin to rely upon one another more—and on the teacher less.

ACCOUNTABILITY

The team members will achieve clarity of purpose by understanding their learning targets and the success criteria. (Refer to the Introduction for teaming term definitions.) Knowing the criteria will also foster individual as well as group accountability. In Figure 2.9, standards, targets, success criteria, and essential questions are all visibly posted and accessible so that students can refer to them often.

Student motivation increases when students begin to track and achieve their learning targets. Frey, Fisher, and Everlove (2009) endorse this view. They posit that once students start to feel more comfortable, to view themselves as productive members of a team, and to see themselves moving toward a clear goal, they become naturally motivated. Thus, accountability

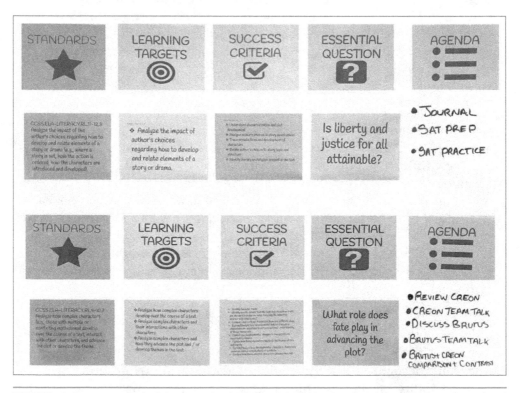

FIGURE 2.9. Example of how a high school teacher made learning targets and success criteria accessible for her students by posting them on the board.

increases both investment of time and motivation. Frey et al. explain, "The reward doesn't have to be external (e.g., grades or praise); learners can intrinsically reward themselves when they experience progress toward an identified goal" (p. 26).

Teams working with clear learning targets and success criteria can determine when a task is complete, and they can also gauge the quality of their own products. For teachers, the challenge arises in setting the learning target high enough on the taxonomy (i.e., to the required levels of thinking complexity) so that the team engages in productive struggle, and in contextualizing the task using real-world applications or situations. We have seen examples where students formulate a problem, then interview outside experts or individuals who would benefit from a solution. Such potential real-world application adds significant meaning and inevitably results in higher engagement with the task. The goal is to ignite students' sense of purpose and their internal motivation to do the work.

Both accountability and productive struggle are necessary ingredients for high cognitive engagement and development. If the task provided to the team does *not* result in productive struggle, then the task is not sufficiently challenging. Teachers should ensure that the team tasks are well designed, encompass the full intent and rigor of the standards, and require high levels of accountability. Teachers should also make sure each student maintains responsibility for reaching his or her own learning targets and that, when appropriate, each student receives an independent grade and not a team grade. The tasks must challenge every member of the team to think and interact with each other—to learn from and with each other, and to be accountable to the team. And the tasks must be relevant and engaging to the team members. A successful and effective team task will likely have some real-world context or application to an issue that is of consequence to students.

STUDENTS TAKE RESPONSIBILITY FOR THEIR WHOLE TEAM

"My biggest success is that my eighth-grade students have learned to hold each other accountable and require teammates to produce evidence of their learning and their progress. In one class, two girls create homework sheets for their teammates who do not typically complete homework, so they will be prepared for upcoming word-stem tests. In many of my 'home' teams, students have set up Instagram group chats to remind each other of deadlines, assigned work, and even to review word stems with each other. Most of my students have taken responsibility for their own learning

---

> *Most of my students have taken responsibility for their own learning and are able to talk about their successes, failures, obstacles, and progress with ease.*

and are able to talk about their successes, failures, obstacles, and progress with ease. Every student has improved as well in the areas of speaking and listening because of the practice they have received by working with their teams this year."

—*Shawn Parks, eighth-grade language arts teacher, Lockerman Middle School, Caroline County, Maryland*

INTERDEPENDENCE

Effective team structure requires that team members use success criteria to give and receive direct feedback from within the team, from other teams, and from the teacher on the work product. Sharing feedback is one of the hallmarks of team interdependence and further solidifies the team's sense of purpose. The shared team task, with clear success criteria, requires team members to rely on one another in generating a product, solution, or decision. As team members work together to accomplish a well-designed team task, they are learning to coach and be coached by peers, which in turn fosters further autonomy and independence from teacher direction.

Van den Bossche, Gijselaers, Segers, and Kirschner's (2006) study of undergraduates identifies interdependence as one of the crucial aspects for engagement in team learning, as well as a factor in the building of mutually shared cognition between team members. Such interdependence, they argue, leads to "higher perceived team effectiveness" (p. 514).

It is important to emphasize that team interdependence is built over time. In the early stage, students are learning from each other and beginning to understand how to provide evidence for their thinking. They are involved in robust and vigorous discussion and debate. Interdependence is built along a continuum. As teams mature with norms and social bonds, and as teachers become more skilled with academic teaming, teachers will begin to design more rigorous tasks that foster interdependence as teams construct their learning. The interdependence of student-led academics teams should be less about the division of work and more about shared reasoning, pushing on each other's thinking, surfacing errors, and revising understanding in the context of peer coaching and support. Tasks that require students to divide the workload in order to learn to work together interdependently may be desirable for larger projects but are not the goal, as they often are in project-based learning. The goal of academic teams is not constructing a shared interdependent product. The goal is to design rigorous-enough learning tasks that push students to *rely on* peer support to reason through various solutions to solve the problem or posed question. The desired effect is peer coaching.

Peer coaching—when team members learn from each other and support one another's learning—is one of the most desirable effects of high-functioning academic teams. The effectiveness of peer coaching has been well documented by research (e.g., Colucci, 2014).

Qualitative studies have also indicated that students respond positively to coaching from their teacher on how to give effective peer feedback and how to assess and incorporate feedback received from peers (Lam, 2010). In our own work in the field, we have seen that time and again when students are given the chance, they are eager to step up and coach each other, often with astonishing positive impacts on academic performance and behavior.

With peer feedback, there is always the chance that students will be confident in their answers while also being incorrect. That is why the teacher must verify the team's learning by checking each student's evidences for the learning target(s). Even with high-functioning teams, the teacher remains the arbiter of learning quality in the classroom through constant verifying and tracking of student and team evidences. If the team has an incorrect answer, the teacher returns the responsibility to the team to figure out where their errors are and to revise their knowledge. If the team remains stuck, they can send out a scout to another team for clues. The teacher is masterfully facilitating the team to increase its self-sufficiency and resilience.

FROM GROUP PROJECTS TO TEAM TASKS

"I have had my eighth-grade students working in groups for over a decade and have long been a proponent of its impact on learning. But by using mini-lessons to teach specific key concepts, and turning the work over to the teams, I have been able to witness how students take responsibility for their own learning. The discussions are rich and tend to be based on more complex ideas than when I originally gave students a task to merely complete together. This, my 26th year of teaching, has been my *best*! I am enthusiastic about getting to school to watch my students progress toward not only my goals for them, but the goals that they have set for themselves."
—*Shawn Parks, eight-grade language arts teacher, Lockerman Middle School, Caroline County, Maryland*

FROM THE CLASSROOM: CREATING AND REINFORCING PURPOSE, ACCOUNTABILITY, AND PRODUCTIVE STRUGGLE

An observer of an eighth-grade English language arts classroom at Lockerman Middle School, in Caroline County, Maryland, shared this experience.

In one eighth-grade class I visited in the spring semester, three boys were sitting together working on a team task. The boys had several texts to read and were trying to find the central idea using textual evidence. The boys were not agreeing with each other. They were interrupting as each was trying to get his point across. The team facilitator said, "Hey guys, do we need to get the talking chips out?"

The team had roles and norms already in place, and the team knew how to interact and communicate effectively. The teacher had placed a resource bin in the middle of their grouped desks that contained supplies as well as supports for teaming, such as question stems and talking chips. At first, she told me, when the team started taking ownership of their learning and really holding each other accountable, they used the supports more frequently. But by this point in the year, they did not need to rely on these supports, like the talking chips, as frequently because they had internalized the concept of equal participation. All the same, having the supports there if they needed to reinforce team expectations was helpful.

As the conversation continued, one boy said to a team member, "I understand what you're trying to say but, that's just weird." That sent the boys into an off-topic conversation on things that were weird. But after about 30 seconds, the team facilitator interjected. "Off topic. We have six minutes." Everyone grabbed his text and got back to the task.

The teacher was not reminding these students of the purpose or that they would be held accountable for the product they produced. She never once told the team to get back on track. She was monitoring the room but allowed the students to *hold each other* accountable. The boys knew the expectations, and the team facilitator knew how to keep the team working. The positive classroom culture, and the clear supports available to the team, were apparent in this classroom.

—*Sara Croll, Learning Sciences International Research and Development*

(See Appendix A for more detailed information on how academic teaming aligns with CASEL's SEL competencies, such as evaluating and self-discipline.)

CREATING AND SUSTAINING A SUPPORTIVE ENVIRONMENT: RECOGNITION, RESOURCES, AND TEACHER COACHING

Enabling Conditions

Defined Team:
- Stability
- Team size
- Diversity

Roles and Clear Norms of Conduct:
- Facilitator and checker
- Respect and accountability

Clear and Compelling Purpose:
- Productive struggle
- Accountability
- Interdependence

A Supportive Environment:
- **Recognition**
- **Resources**
- **Teacher coaching**

FIGURE 2.10. The fourth enabling condition for high-functioning academic teams: a supportive environment.

RECOGNITION AND RESOURCES

Once the teacher has organized teams in the classroom, created and posted foundational team norms and clear roles, and designed challenging team tasks, the next step is to ensure a supportive environment for the team. A supportive environment includes ensuring that all materials the teams need to finish their tasks are readily available, planning ways to offer engaging positive reinforcement or recognitions for team accomplishments, and ensuring that teams get the coaching that they need.

For example, a teacher may devise recognitions and rewards for *team* performance, rather than individual performance. A teacher will also have ensured that students have the necessary foundational knowledge to be ready for the challenging learning task. The teacher also needs to be prepared to genuinely praise and reinforce teams as they fulfill their assigned roles and coach their peers in order to deliver high-quality products that meet the success criteria.

As we visit schools engaged in student-led academic teaming, we have come to recognize that a teacher's personal smile, nod, fist bump, pat on the shoulder, or positive words have a greater impact on developing intrinsic motivation than impersonal awards or stickers on a poster. One of the teacher's roles in academic teaming is to provide constant affirmation and approval as individuals learn and exercise their roles, to ensure that teams move in positive directions, and to let students know clearly when they are on the right track.

We also urge teachers to be careful to avoid competition between teams. Competition can go off the rails in a hurry, damaging the supportive team culture. Student-led academic teams are not competitive, as they might be in a business or sports setting. They are *learning* teams that elevate all students, including those who may need more support to learn. Instead of competition, teams should recognize the effort of their members or the quality of other teams' products. Some techniques for interteam recognition include gallery walks, where teams circulate among other team locations and watch while a representative from each team showcases their work product. Other teams use the success criteria to provide feedback on what was done well and what might be improved.

TEACHER COACHING

Effective teacher coaching of teams depends on honest, immediate, and specific feedback on the team's performance, but feedback strategies should support *team* autonomy, *team* resilience, and *team* purpose. For example, when a team is drifting off course, the teacher might pause the class briefly to remind students of the facilitator's role and to ensure all team members are on task. If that indirect coaching fails, teachers will sometimes take one facilitator aside and coach that individual on strategies to refocus and refresh the team's purpose and norms. Coaching the facilitator, rather than stepping in to act directly, builds and reinforces the team's processes to keep it on track. To understand how best to support and coach a team, teachers can use *root cause analysis*. Educators can ask themselves whether the symptoms they are seeing in a team have the root cause in one of the four enabling conditions (i.e., a *defined team,* with team roles and *clear norms* of conduct, and a compelling *purpose,* in a *supportive environment*).

If one of the four enabling conditions is not present or is insufficient, they may find evidence in the symptoms. Team members may be frustrated, for example, if the learning target and success criteria, or the task directions, are not clear, which would indicate an issue with a *compelling purpose.* Perhaps what looks like an interpersonal conflict on the surface (*norms of conduct*) is really a deeper division in the way the team members see the problem (*compelling purpose*). Or perhaps an individual has been marginalized by other members and is acting out (*norms of conduct*). Was one team member coasting on the work of the others, and was gently corrected by the others, as team norms require? In addition, as teachers walk around tracking evidence that students are progressing to the learning target(s), they can ensure that students have the resources, procedures, and roles in place that students need for team success (the *supporting environment*).

When teachers see an issue in a team, they should give themselves a moment to take stock of the root cause prior to taking action. Any teacher intervention should have a goal to support the *team processes* to work. In other words, teachers should focus all team-related interventions at the team level as much as possible so that the team can then resolve their issue internally, thereby building the team's social and emotional learning skills. The goal is to build the capacity of team members to solve their own issues, just as they will have to do in real life. Teachers are steadily building students' autonomy to operate as a high-functioning team, with as little direct intervention as possible.

This may sound as if teachers are working themselves out of a job, but that is not the case. Teachers remain the ultimate authority in the classroom, even as a master facilitator. Academic teaming grants the gift of readiness for independence to students, and in turn, teachers receive the reward of creating a classroom of scholars who reach higher levels of thinking even while teachers expend less effort. The greatest gift for teachers is time. Teachers can reinvest the time saved on discipline and direct instruction into deeper planning for team tasks and bringing students into the planning process with greater voice and choice. Over time, teachers will want to become ever more skilled in coaching team dynamics.

COACHING FOR SOCIAL-EMOTIONAL LEARNING

Sometimes, the teacher must step in when team conflict becomes personal. One example comes from a fourth-grade classroom in Acreage Pines Elementary School, in Palm Beach County, Florida, where the teacher effectively coached a student team toward increased empathy. We have changed the students' names for privacy reasons. The three boys on the team were marginalizing the only girl on the team, Jane, to the point where Jane began to cry. The teacher pulled Jane aside for less than a minute. Here is a transcript of the video recording:

Jane: "I feel like I'm left out."

Teacher: "Can we go over there, and you can express that feeling to them? Wait, take a moment; gather your thoughts. You have a right to express your feelings, okay? They hurt your feelings, and I want you to tell them that."

Teacher and Jane rejoin the team.

Teacher: "Jane, tell them how you're feeling."

Jane: "Bobby said, 'Jane you're not doing such a good job' and you guys said you agreed with that. And I feel like I'm being left out on everything."

Team member: "Well, Bobby said—"

Teacher: "You can't argue how she's feeling, okay? So, we're going to accept how she's feeling—She's feeling left out. Now my question to you is: What are you going to do to make her feel like she's included? I want you to think about that, okay? Because we're not going to argue about what she's feeling. What she feels, she feels. Okay?"

Team member nods.

Teacher: "All right, so think about how we can help her feel included. Okay, that's for your thoughts. Now, back to what we're doing. I see we have some [textual] support and backings, hmm, but we don't have qualifiers."

Students resume discussion of the team task with participation from all members.

In just minutes, the teacher coached the team through processing the interpersonal conflict and recognizing their peer's feelings, and she pushed them to think about how they would resolve the situation by themselves in the future. Because the teacher coached students to become more aware of their actions, the team was able to increase their social and emotional awareness and their relationship skills. (See Appendix A for more information on how academic teaming addresses CASEL's SEL competencies, such as identifying emotions.)

Effective coaching means teachers create the four enabling conditions for strong teams in the first place and then check to ensure those conditions are maintained. If the enabling conditions are not present, the teacher will spend endless time micromanaging teams, trying to improve their function. A successful launch of student-led teams requires that students have a good understanding of the team's target, task, and success criteria; team roles; awareness of the resources within and outside of the team; and agreement about the basic norms of conduct that will guide the work.

SUPPORTING ACADEMIC TEAMING DEVELOPMENT

As academic teams unfold, teachers will want to consistently look for the four enabling conditions to ensure each is sufficiently in place and will want to search for root causes when teams appear to go astray. Monitoring for team effects cultivates the ground for the teams to progress and to flourish in their academic work.

As we have noted, teachers initially need to ensure that the team's task is clear and that team members know and use the learning targets and success criteria. Students will need to practice their roles. As they practice, the teacher provides feedback while encouraging and nudging the teams to embrace the processes. As students begin to understand norms and expectations, the process of teaming will become more fluent and natural. Once this occurs, social and emotional bonds, such as trust, vulnerability, shared vision and values, tight culture, and empowerment, will form within the collaborative structure of the team. As this happens, the teacher may want to change the focus of feedback from teaming fundamentals to aspects that make for higher-functioning academic teams.

THINGS THAT DERAIL A TEAM:

- Enabling conditions are insufficient or nonexistent.

- The team strives for harmony to the point that differing points of view are held back and the vigorous academic debate that fosters learning is diminished.

- *Mindless* reliance on habitual or scripted routines saps the team's energy and engagement.

- The team lacks individual accountability for learning and enforced norms, which leads to social loafing of members.

- Process loss is when a team is making poor use of its members' roles and strategies for accomplishing the learning task. (Process gain is when the teaming process itself generates more learning than students would have achieved without being in the team structure.)

- Lack of rigorous learning tasks for teams removes challenge and the corresponding cognitive engagement and positive interdependence it creates.

- Teachers intervene and rescue students too early, robbing teams from developing the self-reliance and team culture that comes from social norming and peer support as they practice and develop their social and emotional skills.

- The team cannot overcome student conflict, which requires the teacher to intervene or move members into different teams to get the teams back on track.

RECOGNIZING WHEN TEAMS ARE HIGH-FUNCTIONING—OR NOT

There are certain characteristics teachers can look for to differentiate high-functioning teams from teams that are not there yet. The first is a team's level of effort. Each team member should be expending roughly equal effort to master the learning task, but a high-functioning team also *manages* team effort, employing effective strategies to accomplish the task. For example, effective teams distribute the roles equitably, with attention to team members' strengths; they collaborate and debate, often intensely, but without personal friction; they ensure that each member's point of view is heard; they ensure individual and team accountability for learning and enforcement of norms; and they guard against social loafing that reduces a team's strength.

If teachers see a team whose effort appears to be flagging, they can try encouraging and challenging students to up their game by referring back to their team norms and the teacher's expectations. In the interest of supporting their autonomy, teachers can solicit team members' input on ways to increase their resolve. High-performing teams take pride in the team's work and are self-reliant; that is, members want to do their best for the team. After teams have been launched and are making progress, the teacher continues to monitor to ensure that members do not slip into mindless reliance on habitual routines (one of the dangers of scripted routines for teams), which will rob a team's energy and interest.

The frequency and quality of peer coaching among team members is directly related to how well the team is learning, completing its tasks, and reaching its targets. Authentic peer coaching, where each member is learning from the others, is one of the markers of higher-performing academic teams. While few studies have been conducted on student-to-student peer coaching to improve learning, one 2003 study of high school students who gave and received peer feedback on writing assignments did conclude that peer feedback had a positive effect on student achievement scores (Simmons, 2003). Many of the students in the study had little to no experience in reading and responding to the writing of their peers. At the end of the experiment, a rubric-based portfolio assessment found that students who used peer feedback when revising their writing actually scored higher than students who only used their teacher's comments to revise their writing. Likewise, a great deal of business research on adult peer coaching has shown, as Hackman (2011) notes, ". . . peer coaching was more strongly associated with performance effectiveness than any other factor we assessed in the research" (p. 60).

PEER COACHING BEGINS IN KINDERGARTEN

"We have gotten out of the 'three group rotation' way of teaching. I am able to have one really great lesson that meets all of my students' needs, and I can teach it once. I can tell immediately if my students understand what we are doing, and I can move on or address things as needed. I can step back and let the students do the work. They become the teacher, and they love that. They are so proud of themselves when they are able to help a friend or 'teach' them!"

— *Emily Fazenbaker, kindergarten teacher, Preston Elementary School, Caroline County, Maryland*

SCRIPTED COOPERATIVE LEARNING PROGRAMS MAY LIMIT HIGH PERFORMANCE

We think it is important to note here that the academic teaming model we are describing in this book is *not* a scripted cooperative learning program. Hall (n.d.) explains that "scripted cooperative learning" typically consists of "a controlled interaction between two [or more] students as they learn some body of text material." Although research has found that such scripted cooperative programs may have some learning benefits over students working alone, particularly when it comes to students' recall of material, we believe that when a team operates in a scripted fashion it will have a limiting effect to overall performance in the long term.

The temptation of programs that script student interactions is that it may seem easier to implement a grouping process and avoid "process loss" or time expended while students learn how to interact with each other in a group structure. However tempting this seemingly quicker route might seem, it fails to offer the advantages of authentic academic teaming. Hackman (2011) notes, "although structured techniques assuredly can be effective in lessening a team's exposure to possible process losses, they come at a cost. By limiting or constraining group interaction, they also necessarily cap a team's potential for generating synergistic process gains" (pp. 53–54). The tradeoff is that scripted programs may seem easier to implement, but they can rob the team of the social and emotional learning that comes through the process of developing roles and norming its social bonds. Scripting limits the ownership a team may experience when creating its shared values and culture. Our own observations have reinforced this finding that classrooms where scripted student interactions are practiced cap the potential process gains and cognitive levels that student teams are capable of achieving. Process gains are when students experience greater academic achievement due to the teaming process than they would have experienced otherwise as individual learners not participating in the teaming process.

The goal of student-led academic teaming is to generate the greatest process gains or amount of social, emotional, and cognitive learning of students that comes from the academic teaming process. Like a ladder, the lower rungs are the initial foundation of academic teaming, where social bonds and prosocial skills develop as peers construct their learning together. Students are learning to self-regulate their emotions, develop communication skills, organize, and work together with their roles and norms. The higher rungs of the ladder have greater process gains. To reach the higher rungs, student-led academic teams need to be challenged with rigorous team tasks to engage students in productive struggle. This actually creates two types of productive struggle: (1) cognitive, as students stretch their mental abilities working with their peers to construct their learning; and (2) social and emotional, as students are under increased cognitive demand, they need to develop greater emotional self-control, persistence, leadership, conflict resolution, growth mindset, and empathy as they support one another to achieve the rigorous task. (See Appendices A and B for more detailed information on how academic teaming helps build SEL competencies in all students.)

Although it takes work to form high-functioning academic teams, the social, emotional, and cognitive learning benefits for students are well worth the effort. Chapter 4 reports research findings showing the learning gains that students experience when schools move to student-led academic teams, along with the teacher and student perspectives of the changes. Additional research and case studies, as well as resources and teacher tips, are available on the companion website www.AcademicTeaming.com.

REFLECTION QUESTIONS FOR EVIDENCE OF HIGH-FUNCTIONING TEAMS

As teachers reflect on the progress they are making toward student-led academic teaming, they may find their answers to the following questions useful:

1. What percentage of your daily classroom time is spent on direct instruction?

2. What percentage of your students can assess their own learning each day?

3. How do your students verify and track the learning of their teammates?

4. How do you support student team members to peer coach each other?

5. How often are students able to respond to the needs and regulate the behaviors of their teammates?

6. How often does students' voice and choice influence lesson planning and task design that allows them to explore real-world connections of interest to them?

7. Do students monitor their own norms, routines, and roles?

8. Are students using academic language in their team talk?

9. How do you determine the pace of lessons? How often does student evidence help determine lesson pacing?

10. Does most of your feedback go to individual students or to student teams?

11. How often is your feedback given in the moment during a lesson versus after the fact?

12. Do student team members translate team feedback into action for learning?

13. On a scale of 1 to 4, how would you rate the overall learning autonomy of your students?

14. On a scale of 1 to 4, how would you rate the level of trust between you and your students, and between students and students?

15. Do students exemplify SEL skills such as empathy, constructive disagreement, and self-actualization?

16. Is collaboration and academic safety the dominant culture of the classroom?

📄 POINTS TO CONSIDER: CHAPTER 2

This page is to jot down points from Chapter 2 to consider later and discuss with colleagues and students.

_____

_____

_____

_____

_____

_____

_____

_____

_____

_____

_____

_____

_____

_____

_____

_____

_____

_____

_____

_____

_____

_____

_____

⮧ WHAT'S COMING

Chapter 3 explains the neuroscience behind academic teaming. We include research that supports the idea that when students work together, they can better remember what they learned, make better decisions, and increase their attention control. We also examine how academic teaming develops social-emotional growth and problem-solving skills in all students and how it addresses personalized learning and cultural diversity.

CHAPTER 3:

NEUROSCIENCE AND OTHER RESEARCH SUPPORT FOR ACADEMIC TEAMING

We noted in the Introduction that educational neuroscience is a new field of study that examines the findings from neuroscience, cognitive psychology, and pedagogy to determine if they can be translated into educational practice. The more we discover about how the brain learns, the more likely we are to make decisions in curricula and instruction that will result in greater student achievement. Some strategies that teachers have been using for a long time, such as authentic cooperative learning and Socratic questioning, have been successful because they are compatible with the neural processing that occurs during learning. They were approaches that worked, even though we did not know at the time *why* they were so effective. That is exactly what makes the discoveries in educational neuroscience so exciting. They are explaining the *why!*

RESEARCH SUPPORT FOR TEAMING

Research findings in several areas of neuroscientific inquiry have suggested why brains working together are often more effective at solving problems than brains working alone. Let us explore some of these findings.

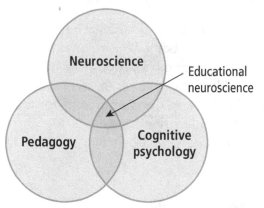

FIGURE 3.1. The diagram shows that the research fields of neuroscience, cognitive psychology, and pedagogy contribute to the new field of study called educational neuroscience.

BRAINS WITHIN A TEAM CAN SYNCHRONIZE

One fascinating research result was that the brain waves of some team members may synchronize while they are trying to solve a problem (Szymanski et al., 2017). Using electroencephalography (EEG), researchers found that those team members whose brain waves began to synchronize with each other were able to make quicker decisions and solve a problem more efficiently than those members whose brain waves did not synchronize. This result may explain why some teams perform better than others.

COLLABORATION INCREASES BRAIN SYNCHRONY

A similar EEG study found that the more team members collaborated with each other during problem solving, the more their brain waves became synchronized (Hu et al., 2018). This finding demonstrates the importance of keeping academic teams together for an extended period if they are working on a major project. Collaboration does not come easy, especially in classrooms with a student population diverse in native languages, cultures, socio-economic backgrounds, and abilities.

TALKING ABOUT NEW LEARNING HELPS THE LEARNER REMEMBER IT

Talk is one of the most powerful memory devices. Adding the auditory modality increases the number of brain regions that process the new learning. Student-led academic teaming encourages participants to share their ideas verbally with other team members. One study showed that when students talked about what they learned in school in science that day with a parent, their memory of the new learning was accurate six days later (Leichtman et al., 2017). Speaking about what one is learning is sometimes called the production effect, and a number of studies have shown that it is a significant aid to long-term memory (MacLeod, Gopie, Hourihan, Neary, & Ozubko, 2010).

TEAMS MAKE BETTER COGNITIVE DECISIONS THAN INDIVIDUALS

As team members work together, social and emotional bonds strengthen, and mutual trust emerges that can affect a team member's decision making. For instance, one typical study found that as team members brought additional pertinent information to the group, individual members were persuaded to change their own decisions so that the final group decision was better than any single one offered by an individual member (Penczynski, 2016). Once again, it takes time to build trust in a group, but it can be a powerful force in academic team learning.

STUDENT-LED ACADEMIC TEAMS ENHANCE POSITIVE SOCIAL-EMOTIONAL GROWTH

Studies have shown for a long time that emotions enhance long-term memory (Fastenrath et al., 2014). A small almond-shaped structure called the amygdala, located deep in the brain's emotional (limbic)

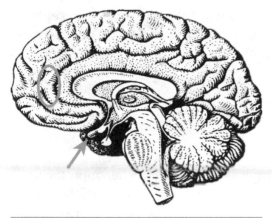

area, is responsible for encoding emotional responses into long-term memory. Meanwhile, another set of neurons, called mirror neurons, are developing in the adolescent brain (see Figure 3.2). Mirror neurons are responsible for empathy and directing one's social interactions.

FIGURE 3.2. In this cross-section view of the left hemisphere, the arrow points to the amygdala and the oval shows the location of the mirror neurons.

Schools have always placed heavy emphasis on a student's cognitive growth, assuming that care for social and emotional growth would occur in the home. However, research in neuroscience has clearly found that social and emotional growth have a significant impact on one's cognitive development. That is because the emotional and social regions of the brain are closely connected to the cognitive centers that process information. This realization has prompted educators in recent years to look for ways that schools can positively contribute to their students' social and emotional growth. It also explains why we have called our teaming model SECL. From what we understand about the brain, cognitive growth is heavily dependent on one's social and emotional interactions.

Strategies that target social and emotional growth aim to improve students' ability to self-regulate emotions, handle adversity, encourage care and respect for others, and make responsible decisions. When properly implemented, studies show that these strategies reduce discipline problems and emotional distress while improving prosocial behavior (Portnow et al., 2018). A meta-analysis of numerous studies found that when schools pay attention to social and emotional growth, student achievement increases (Corcoran et al., 2018).

Student-led academic teaming supports social-emotional growth, although the dynamics can be quite complex, especially if it is a culturally and linguistically diverse group. Team members dealing with an emotionally charged learning target may be at various stages of social and emotional maturity. Their tolerance for differing views may vary widely as well as their degree of participation in decision making. During discussions, the emotional and rational areas of the brain of each team member are assessing the opinions of other team members to determine if they are acceptable or need to be moderated. When used regularly, student-led academic teaming can be very helpful in developing acceptable social and emotional behaviors. This is particularly important now because teenagers are spending more time than ever with digital devices and less time interacting with real people.

STUDENT-LED ACADEMIC TEAMS MAKE BETTER SOCIAL-EMOTIONAL DECISIONS THAN INDIVIDUALS

Studies show that if the learning target is clear and teacher monitoring is consistent, then the norms of acceptable social and emotional behaviors will usually guide the team to a positive outcome. In other words, as the team does its work over time, the variance among individual opinions and stages of social and emotional development tend to migrate toward a group decision that is more rational than the decision of any individual (Kugler, Kausel, & Kocher, 2013).

STUDENT-LED ACADEMIC TEAMING HELPS DEVELOP COLLABORATIVE PROBLEM-SOLVING SKILLS

Results from the 2015 Program for International Student Assessment (PISA) that tested the collaborative problem-solving skills of 15-year-olds show that the United States ranked 11th out of the 51 countries that participated (Organization for Economic Cooperation and Development [OECD], 2017). However, only 14 percent of the US students achieved level 4, which is the highest level of complexity in the test. A good deal of the work in student-led academic teaming involves team members collaborating to solve complex problems. Regular practice with these skills builds and strengthens the neural networks responsible for higher-order thinking as well as the social networks that support collaborative interactions.

STUDENT-LED ACADEMIC TEAMING SUPPORTS VISIBLE LEARNING

In recent years, John Hattie's (2012) ongoing meta-analyses on the many factors that influence student achievement have raised interest in what Hattie calls "visible learning." This approach involves teachers seeing learning through the eyes of students, whereas students see teaching as the essential component to their continuing learning. Hattie maintains that when learning is visible, then the student knows what to do and how to do it, and the teacher knows whether learning is occurring. Teachers should continually look for evidence of the impact their actions are having on their students' thinking and products and should use this evidence to decide if instructional changes are needed.

The latest set of factors affecting student learning and achievement includes 1,200 meta-analyses and lists 195 of these factors (Hattie, 2015). We noted earlier that the factors are rated using a statistical measurement called effect size. Recall that effect size quantifies the size of the effect that an intervention has on the experimental group; effect sizes of 0.1 to 0.3 are small, 0.4 to 0.6 are medium, and 0.71 are large. The symbol for effect size is d.

A review of Hattie's list shows the effect sizes of some of the factors that are inherent in the student-led academic teaming process (see Figure 3.3). For instance, the team's work includes feedback (d 5 0.73), self-questioning (d 5 0.64), problem solving (d 5 0.63), study skills (d 5 0.60), peer tutoring (d 5 0.55), cooperative work (d 5 0.55), and peer influences (d 5 0.53). Another component, the teacher's estimate of student achievement of a task, has an impressive effect size of 1.62. As student-led academic teams are working, teachers have ample opportunities to track learning through their students' eyes by listening to their discussions, by asking specific questions about their thinking, and by examining the team's results. As we discussed in Chapters 1 and 2, this evidence helps the teacher to decide whether to reteach a topic, ask pertinent "what if" questions, give additional directions to the team, or assess their final results and move on.

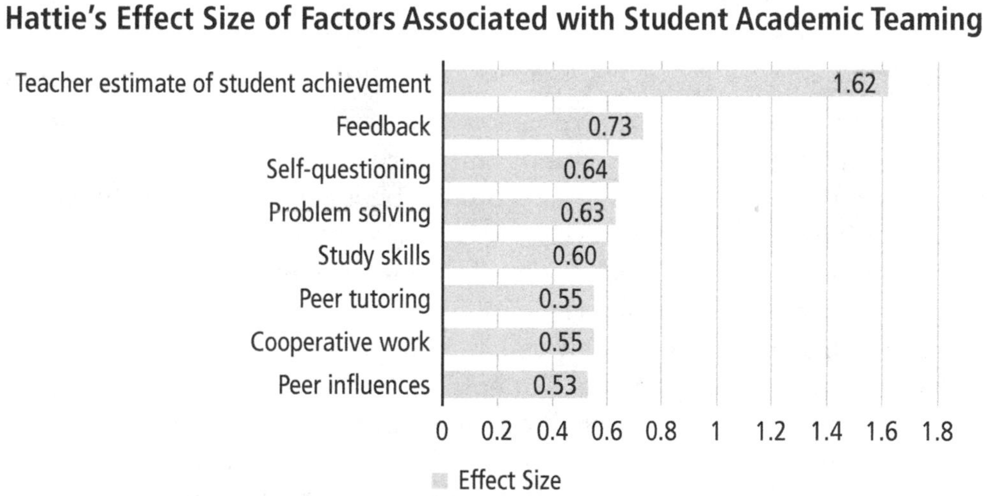

Hattie's Effect Size of Factors Associated with Student Academic Teaming

FIGURE 3.3. The chart shows the effect sizes of some of the factors associated with student-led academic teaming. Effect sizes from 0.40 to 0.60 are considered as having a medium effect, and greater values are considered as having a large effect. (Adapted from Hattie, 2015.)

STUDENT-LED ACADEMIC TEAMING SUPPORTS PERSONALIZED LEARNING

The increased use of technology in schools has prompted some educators to suggest that technology makes it easier to optimize the pace of learning and instructional approach to the needs of each learner. They call this *personalized learning*, a term resurrected from the 1960s that remains poorly defined among educators today. Proponents say that in this era of technology, learning can be tailored to meet the individual interests, strengths, and needs of students while giving them a voice and choice in their learning. They can accomplish their learning targets by getting the necessary information and appropriate feedback from software, the Internet, and other information sources. Critics argue that this initiative is more about selling technology products than reforming and improving instructional practice. The term itself lacks clarity, and the guidelines for implementing it vary considerably. As a result, it is difficult to find any reliable research to support it (Herald, 2017).

Earlier in this book, we expressed our concerns about the adverse impact that overuse of technology is having by rewiring students' brains in areas vital to learning. Furthermore, relying mainly on technology as the major information source does not mean that students will get a deep understanding of the concept, nor understand its application to the real world. In fact, they may not even process the learning. For instance, before digital devices were so readily available, students had to use their *own* brains to solve a "what if" question posed by the teacher. Now, they often go directly to the Internet to discover how *others* have solved the "what if" questions. As a consequence, their brains are getting little practice in higher-order thinking and creative problem solving—competencies identified as essential 21st-century skills.

This practice of turning to the Internet to handle information rather than to one's own brain may explain why research studies suggest that the capacity of working memory—the temporary memory where immediate processing occurs—is decreasing in younger people who proactively reduce the cognitive load in their working memory (Wiemers & Redick, 2018). The long-standing accepted capacity of working memory was five to seven items. More recent studies place the capacity for younger students today at only three to four items. Why does that matter? Beginning readers, for example, rely heavily on working memory to hold on to the words at the beginning of a sentence so that a complete thought is formed when the reader gets to the end of the sentence. If the capacity of working memory is decreasing, then words at the beginning of the sentence fall out of working memory and the reader cannot make sense of the sentence. Moreover, learners also rely on working memory to hold enough different ideas simultaneously to determine how they may link together to form a larger concept—the key to deep understanding (Wang, Ren, & Schweizer, 2017).

Rather than get involved in what personalized learning means—or doesn't mean—we know that student-led academic teams can be designed to first, use technology strategically and second, collaborate so that the interests, strengths, and needs of each team member can be met over time. To us, personalized learning means that the team members and teachers are working together and are *personally interacting* with each other to ensure that all members of the team successfully accomplish the learning targets.

STUDENT-LED ACADEMIC TEAMING DEVELOPS SUSTAINED ATTENTION

For several years, research studies have revealed that the average adolescent spends only a few seconds with a site on a digital device to determine whether that site is of interest; otherwise, the viewer moves on. The individual's brain is being trained to make a decision in just a few seconds as to whether the information on a site will capture and sustain the viewer's attention (Giedd, 2012). Even action video games do not encourage sustained attention (Trisolini, Petilli, & Daini, 2018). However, significant decisions on important real-world problems cannot be made in several seconds. Critical thinking, problem solving, and creativity take time and sustained attention—important components of persistence—a required 21st-century skill (also recall the Harvard SEL competencies in the Introduction chapter).

This is just one more reason to focus and limit the use of technology to strategic purposes in student-led academic teams. In academic teams, students spend considerable time discussing and analyzing their new learning face-to-face. Texting is generally not permitted. They focus on a deeper understanding and the application of their learning to real-world situations. Time is also spent exploring ways to connect their new learning to what they already know so as to expand and strengthen existing neural networks and create new ones. The regular use of teams working face-to-face provides the distributed practice that young people need to develop sustained attention and to remember what they have learned.

STUDENT-LED ACADEMIC TEAMING ADDRESSES CULTURAL DIVERSITY

School populations in the United States are becoming more culturally diverse than ever before. Culture shapes our perception of who we are and where we fit in our family, community, and society. By understanding our own culture, we gain a greater appreciation for how to interact with those whose culture is different from ours, both in and out of school. Teachers should select instructional strategies that strive to help students develop an understanding of the perspectives of their peers with different cultural backgrounds and learn to function successfully in a multiethnic and multicultural environment.

In academic teaming, students work together in a give-and-take environment. They each play the role of student and teacher throughout the collaborative process. In this way, they can learn about the customs and beliefs of other cultures, thereby fostering tolerance and acceptance in the school and community. By working toward a common learning target, team members develop an understanding of the behavior of other students in the appropriate cultural context. This helps them to know differing viewpoints and perspectives and how to respond to these situations.

Such experiences are particularly important for teenagers because their brains' social neurons are maturing at a rapid pace. They are networking with the brain's emotional system to learn and develop appropriate behaviors when interacting with individuals from diverse cultures.

TEACHERS ALSO BENEFIT FROM TEAMING

Teaching can be a lonely profession. There are rare opportunities for teachers to collaborate with each other and share experiences during the school day, and there are only a few times to do so during the school year. Teaming with teachers is more complicated than with children and teenagers. Adults have already developed a deeply held set of values and morals that guides their behavior and thinking. Changing adults' opinions is a lot more difficult, as is getting them to understand views that are the opposite of theirs. Yet, recent research shows that teachers working in teams can learn more than teachers working alone, and they can more easily solve difficult problems, especially if there are teacher leaders facilitating the process (Bouwmans, Runhaar, Wesselink, & Mulder, 2017). In Chapter 5, we further discuss creating communities of practice for teachers and school leaders around academic teaming.

📄 **POINTS TO CONSIDER: CHAPTER 3**

This page is to jot down points from Chapter 3 to consider later and discuss with colleagues and students.

_____

_____

_____

_____

_____

_____

_____

_____

_____

_____

_____

_____

_____

_____

_____

_____

_____

_____

_____

_____

_____

_____

_____

_____

⤳ WHAT'S COMING

In Chapter 4, we offer case studies of schools in a district that has implemented academic teaming over a period of one to three years. These studies encompass schools of varying sizes with a variety of student demographics and unique challenges. We examine data from the Learning Sciences Applied Research Center's groundbreaking study that shows evidence of academic teaming narrowing achievement gaps. We also include perspectives from educators who have witnessed students transform into engaged, confident classroom leaders as a result of academic teaming.

CHAPTER 4:

STUDENT-LED ACADEMIC TEAMING RESULTS

The research report and educator experiences in this chapter describe the positive impact of student-led academic teaming in the Des Moines Public Schools district, where 22 of the 64 schools made the shift to academic teaming. A research study of this scale—with student data that meet rigorous research standards—is one of the largest of its kind for this new instructional model.

This chapter features case studies of one elementary school and two high schools from the research study, but these are only three of many schools across the nation that are successfully implementing academic teaming. Elementary, middle, and high schools from both urban and rural communities in small, medium, and large districts have all found that shifting to academic teaming resulted in *increased student achievement, authentic social-emotional learning, and improved student behavior*. We include further case studies and research reports on www.AcademicTeaming.com from schools in Grand Island, Nebraska; Caroline County, Maryland; and Pinellas County, Florida, among others. Despite the distinct challenges each school and district faces—from influxes of nonnative speakers to high poverty and seemingly intractable behavior problems—academic teaming has proven to be a positive transformation for students and educators, who report both academic growth and constructive social, emotional, and cognitive impacts.

The Des Moines Public Schools district partnered with Learning Sciences International to implement student-led academic teaming through the Schools for Rigor initiative, which includes the following components:

- ❖ Schoolwide implementation of the student-led academic teaming instructional model, designed to ensure rigorous academics, build social-emotional and 21st-century skills, and fully support learning aligned to standards in every classroom

- ❖ Professional development for school leaders and classroom staff to help them successfully make the shift to a new model of teaching and learning and achieve deep and sustained results

- ❖ Intensive coaching for leaders and teachers and supporting technology to gauge the implementation, including Rigor Diagnostic and

RigorWalk® on Trend Tracker® to gauge schoolwide implementation, LSI Standards Tracker® for teachers to verify and track student evidences, and LSI Growth Tracker® as a peer coaching and academic teaming techniques micro-credentialing platform

DES MOINES PUBLIC SCHOOLS: NARROWING THE ACHIEVEMENT GAP—DES MOINES, IOWA

With 64 schools, the Des Moines Public Schools district is the largest school district in Iowa. In the 2017–18 school year, 35 of these schools qualified for Title I School Improvement funds. Because student subgroups failed to achieve Adequate Yearly Progress in accordance with the Elementary and Secondary Education Act, the Iowa Department of Education designated many of these 35 schools as "Schools in Need of Assistance."

Des Moines Public Schools Associate Superintendent Matt Smith takes pride in serving a diverse student population. "We are a majority minority school district," he says. "The city of Des Moines is a refugee resettlement community, and so we have students from all over the world. Well over a hundred different languages are spoken in our community and in our hallways." The English language learner student population across the district has exploded over the past few decades. According to the district:

> Since 1990, the number of English Language Learners [ELLs] in Des Moines Public Schools has grown by 700 percent, from less than 1,000 students in 1990–91 to more than 6,800 students in 2016–17. During this period the overall student enrollment remained stable between 32,000 and 33,000 students. ELL students in Des Moines Public Schools now constitute more than one out of five of our enrollment and account for nearly one quarter of the total number of ELL students in Iowa. (Des Moines Public Schools, n.d.-a)

District administrators knew that equity and access had to become a major focus if the district hoped to narrow the achievement gap for student subgroups and to ensure all students had access to an excellent education. In a report about Des Moines Public School's partnership with the Wallace Foundation and Learning Sciences International, Smith was quoted describing the collective vision for the district: "All 33,000 of the students who come to us deserve the same opportunities no matter where they come from or what they come with" (Des Moines Public Schools, 2016).

In 2016, Des Moines Public Schools partnered with Learning Sciences International to begin implementation of Schools for Rigor with six schools. A year later, 16 additional schools also became Schools for Rigor. In 2018–19—

Des Moines Public School District's third year of implementation—the district is in the process of expanding the initiative to seven more schools. Thus, nearly half the schools in the district are implementing academic teaming as part of the Schools for Rigor initiative. Superintendent Tom Ahart's vision is for the Des Moines Public Schools district to become the model for urban education in the United States.

HOWE ELEMENTARY SCHOOL

HOWE'S DEMOGRAPHICS

Student Population: 308
Number of Teachers: 26
Free and Reduced Price Lunch: 85%
Special Education: 9%
English Language Learners: 32%
White: 35%
Black: 18%
Hispanic: 35%
Asian: 4%
Two or More Races: 7%
Native Hawaiian or Pacific Islander: ,1%
American Indian/Alaska Native: ,1%

Howe Elementary School is in its third year of Schools for Rigor implementation. Howe is a Title I school where students face many challenges in their personal lives. In the 2017–18 school year, 85 percent qualified for free and reduced price lunch. Thirty-two percent of Howe's students were English language learners. Howe students deal with trauma, homelessness, low socio-economic households, and problems with US Immigration and Customs Enforcement. About a quarter of the student population were transient. Despite its relatively small size of 308 students, the school required its own full-time mental health counselor. To cope with these stressful circumstances, and to be able to learn effectively, students needed to build resiliency.

A NEW COMMITMENT TO INSTRUCTIONAL TRANSFORMATION

Before joining Schools for Rigor, Howe Elementary Principal Jill Burke already knew she wanted to lead instructional transformation. She has been at Howe for six years and says the staff have always worked hard to serve their students and ensure equitable outcomes. But despite their efforts, the school was still not seeing results.

> We always had staff members trying to do their best, pulling in different instructional strategies. But our focus was always on the teacher. When either the instructional coaches or I would go into the classrooms, we were looking at what the teacher was doing to gauge whether they were successful. I did look at student engagement, but I didn't really look at the student evidence of learning or what the students were doing. I wasn't providing teachers with feedback that could get better results for kids. Reviewing our data in Professional Learning Communities (PLCs), when only 50 percent of the kids got it, we'd still move on. So, we were working really hard, but not getting results no matter what we did. We'd see a pocket, maybe a little bit of change here or a little bit of change there, but it never carried over to *all* kids, and the changes weren't consistent throughout the school from year to year.

Burke visited a School for Rigor—Acreage Pines Elementary in Palm Beach County, Florida—and knew she wanted her students to experience the level of academic rigor she saw in Acreage Pines's team-centered classrooms:

> Once I had the opportunity to walk those classrooms and see what I saw, I couldn't walk away and say, "I think I'll pass, I think we're fine." I wanted to learn, and I wanted to be better. I thought I was a good instructional leader, but I guess I didn't know what being an instructional leader meant.

Burke was excited when the district presented her with the opportunity for Howe to become a School for Rigor, where teachers could implement student-led academic teaming in every classroom. As Burke rolled out the initiative, teachers began to see the potential of academic teaming to address equity and access and to narrow stubborn learning gaps that Howe had struggled with for years.

EQUITY AND ACCESS FOR ALL

Howe had worked on the issue of equity and access before, but Burke acknowledges that there had been little root cause analysis of why certain subgroups were struggling. Burke and her staff were not sure of the best way to use student data to make adjustments to instruction. Burke says, "We really didn't show any growth or closing of any gaps." Instruction was not meeting the needs of all students at Howe.

Associate Superintendent Matt Smith emphasizes that equity is not built into traditional models of instruction:

> The traditional pedagogy of having students sit in rows and just listen as the spectators of their own learning didn't allow for students to interact with their peers and learn about the differences and uniqueness their peers bring to the table. The traditional instructional design in many

Equity must be in the instructional design, not only in the curriculum.

cases was actually punitive towards students for talking and sharing, because that was considered disruptive. Equity must be in the instructional design, not only in the curriculum.

The Des Moines Public Schools district created an equity framework around three key areas: learning, thriving, and belonging. Burke says that once Howe began to implement academic teaming she felt that students were hitting these key areas without needing to focus on the equity framework explicitly:

> What we've noticed is more conversations and more kids engaged. These kids feel like they're part of something. It's not necessarily that we focus on the equity framework. I think that the equity framework just flows through. My teachers can instantly see if the kids are not getting it, and they're able to adjust the instruction and ask our coaches for new strategies. Most of our PLC time is now centered around conversations about specific kids or specific demographics and helping them achieve their targets. We're no longer waiting to receive our state test results. Now we have student information day-to-day; teaming changes the way we instruct, assess, track, teach, and collect student evidence from our kids. Teaming allows every student to be part of a group, allows every student to have a voice, and allows every student to have the opportunity for productive struggle.

Teaming allows every student to be part of a group, allows every student to have a voice, and allows every student to have the opportunity for productive struggle.

(See Appendix E for more detailed information on how academic teaming aligns to equity principles, such as adapting to student needs to drive improvement and building student agency.)

But how does academic teaming work for students who might not be comfortable speaking, such as English language learners or introverts, or students with behavior problems? "Do we want our kids to stay in their comfort zones?" Burke asks. "We'd be setting those kids up for failure later on by saying they're not able to work in a team."

> We can't say to our students, "You aren't able to do this task because your language skills are too low," or "You aren't capable of working in a group because you can't sit still with your classmates." If we think like that, then we have already decided our students' limitations, and that's not fair. Our best learning happens in a situation where we're not comfortable, where we have to do something different than we've ever done before. As teachers we have to be advocates for our students and not allow them to fall right into their safe zone. One of our ELL students recently said, "I can learn so much better when a teammate tells me because I hear a different way." If we'd pigeonholed this student in her comfort zone, I'm not sure that she would have gotten what she deserved out of her educational experiences.

We have to be advocates for our students and not allow them to fall right into their safe zone.

Although teachers might have to push reluctant students and support them through the challenges of working in academic teams at first, Associate Superintendent Matt Smith believes students need to learn to help each other. "A network of peer support *has to exist* amongst our students—the responsibility of providing support can't just be on the shoulders of the teacher. That's far too big of a burden for teachers to bear."

> *The responsibility of providing support can't just be on the shoulders of the teacher. That's far too big of a burden for teachers to bear.*

Working in teams, Smith says, teaches students to support each other as they autonomously develop relationship skills, self-awareness, and prosocial mindsets, all aspects of social, emotional, and cognitive learning (SECL). Teaming also allows students to express their diverse identities. (See Appendix A for more detailed information on how academic teaming aligns to CASEL's SEL competencies, such as perspective-taking and appreciating diversity.)

> Students not only support one another academically, they also support one another socially and emotionally. Our students feel validated and affirmed about who they are as individuals, and they are also creating and developing a sense of empathy and compassion for one another. Within their academic teams, students are empowered to recognize and speak their identities.

In fact, Smith argues that students can support each other in ways their teachers might never be able to:

> As educators, we are used to bringing our perspective to the curriculum instead of asking students to make their own connections and bring their own relevance into the learning. With the diversities we have within our student body in Des Moines, each student's perspective is so unique even when they live in the same neighborhoods. Students can learn so much from one another about their struggles and their successes and about how policies and practices impact them. Teaming allows students to take the academic content and create real-life applications while they're connecting with their peers at a level of depth they never have before.

> *Teaming allows students to take the academic content and create real-life applications while they're connecting with their peers at a level of depth they never have before.*

HOWE KINDERGARTEN ACHIEVEMENT GAP DROPS TO ZERO

Like all the teachers at Howe Elementary, kindergarten teacher Julie Lake had students who entered her classroom each year not speaking a word of English. Some had never been to preschool or childcare, so they also lacked social-emotional skill development. Before the Schools for Rigor Initiative began in 2016, many of Lake's students were failing to reach their expected growth goals.

As Howe began implementing Schools for Rigor in 2016–17, Lake gradually began to shift her kindergarten classroom from the traditional teacher-centered model to student-led academic teaming. Just a year later, in the second year of the initiative, 100 percent of Lake's students met or exceeded their expected growth on the state MAP® Growth™ 2017–18 assessment. Lake says that in her 12 years teaching kindergarten at Howe, she has never seen her students reach the level of cognitively complex learning they are now achieving. Lake credits teaming for allowing *all* of her students to access academically rigorous content:

We're always having to make things more rigorous at more complex levels because the kids are just moving along a lot faster. I believe it's because they're doing all the problem solving and they're working in teams.

Since we started Schools for Rigor, our kindergarten scores here at Howe have been the highest in the district. And last year, I believe, the highest in the state. One hundred percent of our kids met their expected growth for the last two years. Usually, I have a section of kids who are working on getting it, kids who got it, and then a little group of kids who have high achievement and high growth. In the last two years, the group of kids who are way above the expected growth is so much bigger. So, we're always having to make things more rigorous at more complex levels because the kids are just moving along a lot faster. I believe it's because they're doing all the problem solving and they're working in teams.

Lake says that academic teaming helped her realize what her kindergarten students were capable of and allowed her students to learn at

Summary data by subject

	Mathematics
Percentage of Students who Met or Exceeded their Projected RIT	100.0%
Percentage of Projected Growth Met	225.4%
Count of Students with Growth Projection Available and Valid Beginning and Ending Term Scores	22
Count of Students who Met or Exceeded their Projected Growth	22
Median Conditional Growth Percentile	99

FIGURE 4.1. Julie Lake's kindergarten class, state MAP® Growth™ assessment math scores Fall 2017 to Spring 2018 (their second year of Schools for Rigor).

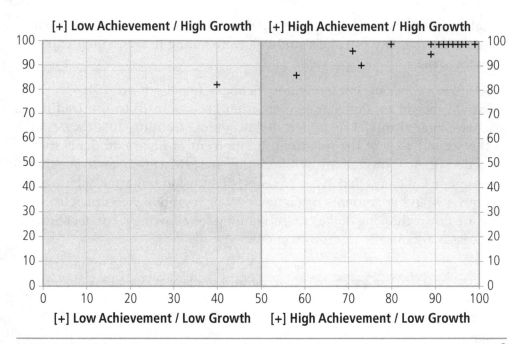

FIGURE 4.2. Julie Lake's kindergarten class—individual student growth, state MAP® Growth™ assessment math scores Fall 2017 to Spring 2018 (their second year of Schools for Rigor). Note that all students reached high growth, and nearly every student reached high achievement.

higher taxonomy levels than before. Now Lake has high expectations for all her students.

> I think that they're so much more capable because they're working in teams. My tracking is easier because I can see my students working through problems, and I can hear them talking. I can teach them at higher taxonomy levels: instead of saying, "Okay, here's your sight word. Go to your desk and write it down," now it's more like, "Hey, your team is responsible for coming up with a sentence using this sight word"—and they do it! They can do these more rigorous tasks now because they're working with their teams. For example, they're not afraid to pick up books and read. It used to be me reading a book and then discussing the characters and the setting with them. Now, they're in their teams and they're pulling the main idea and the key details and reading nonfiction. It's just really incredible.

Lake's classroom was not the only one to reap such amazing benefits from academic teaming. According to Principal Jill Burke, "In our kindergarten and first grade classes, we show almost a zero gap between any of our students, which is a huge accomplishment, especially with our kids being all over the board when they enter school." Howe Elementary is closing the gap in SECL for all students.

In our kindergarten and first grade classes we now show almost a zero gap between any of our students, which is a huge accomplishment, especially with our kids being all over the board when they enter school.

BEHAVIOR IMPROVES AS ACADEMIC TEAMING TAKES OFF

Educators at Howe noticed that academic teaming had a big impact on students' behavior. "Our behavior referrals went down tremendously last year," says Principal Jill Burke, "and I'm not surprised, because the kids are more engaged and on board. When there are more deliberate tasks, and the teacher is monitoring the teaming, it's so much easier to create an accommodation or adaptation to prevent behavior problems."

First-grade teacher Allison Berg made a deliberate choice to turn one student's strong personality into an asset by making him a leader in his team, which led to a dramatic decrease in his negative behaviors.

> One student in my classroom has a very strong personality and struggles with negative behavior. Being part of a team allows his personality to shine through in a positive way. He had been very bossy towards other students, so I knew he needed to have the facilitator role in his team. Sometimes I huddle my facilitator students together and ask them what it means to be a good facilitator. He was able to tell me that a good facilitator leads the group but doesn't tell their teammates what to do. He has shown so much growth and improved his negative behavior more than I think he would have in a traditional classroom. He's stepped up into a leadership position, and the other two members in his triad group really look up to him. Even when we're doing individualized tasks, they ask him for help because they see him as a leader in the classroom. I tell him I hope he continues to be a good role model for the other facilitators, and he has been.

Since Berg did not have to put as much time into regulating his behavior, she could instead focus on rigorous academics. As a black male, this student's academic success is especially critical considering the Des Moines Public School District's commitment to what they call the WIG, or "wildly important goal," of making sure that in three years their black male data is at or above all the other subgroups. (See Appendix A for more detailed information on how academic teaming aligns with CASEL's SEL competencies, such as respect for others and social engagement.)

Academic teaming has completely changed her learning in the classroom. Her scores have gone up, and she can communicate so much better. Now instead of acting out and being disruptive and not concentrating on her learning, she is a leader. She's a student I can count on.

Fourth-grade teacher Rebecca Studer also saw one of her most challenging students grow into a leader.

One of my students—who comes from a low poverty, not very stable home was very disruptive and didn't want to do anything when I had her in second grade. Now, having her in my fourth-grade class, she has taken on the leadership role I modeled. She is stepping up to organize her team and makes sure everybody understands their roles. Academic teaming has completely changed her learning in the classroom. Her scores have gone up, and she can communicate so much better. Now instead of acting out and being disruptive and not concentrating on her learning, she is a leader. She's a student I can count on.

Teacher Julie Lake also notes that she can focus more on academics because she does not have to spend as much time and effort on discipline in her kindergarten classroom.

I don't have a behavior chart in my room anymore. At the beginning of the year my students and I talked about "above the line" behavior and "below the line" behavior. I just have to say, "Are you above the line or below the line?" Basically, we have no negative behaviors unless it's a special circumstance. I believe it's because they're in their teams and they're allowed to talk all day. This is my third year now without any sort of behavior chart. I'm not monitoring for behavior anymore. I'm tracking for learning, which is a great thing.

> *This is my third year now without any sort of behavior chart. I'm not monitoring for behavior anymore. I'm tracking for learning, which is a great thing.*

STUDENTS RECOGNIZE THEIR GROWTH

Howe Elementary students are perceiving the positive effects of academic teaming themselves. Burke notes that when her students transfer to other schools, sometimes she will get an email from the new school that says, "You'll never believe it but they ask: are we still going to work in teams?" Since there are now 29 Schools for Rigor in Des Moines Public Schools, sometimes the answer is *yes*. Burke says kids are excited when they get to continue teaming because "they know that they get the opportunity to talk, to share, to push each other's thinking, to struggle productively."

When students transfer into Howe Elementary from a school not using academic teaming, they notice the difference in their learning. One fourth-grade student who transferred into Howe says, "I feel like I'm learning more here because with group work there's more ideas and more different opinions and then you can learn more from those opinions sometimes."

Another fourth-grade student says, "I'm glad we work in teams now because it helps me learn. We can think out loud instead of keeping thoughts inside, and you can tell people why you think that and why you disagree."

A classmate agrees that the support of her teammates helps her feel less stressed and better able to access the content.

> Our peers help us learn because if we're stuck on something, if you just ask your peers, they will help you. If we're alone, it does put pressure on us. But if we're with a group, it's easier because you don't feel so stressed if you can't get something because you have people around you.

Being part of a team with peer support, well-defined norms, clear expectations, and resources designed for autonomy makes students feel less frustrated and empowers them to depend less on the teacher for learning: "We all make mistakes, and that just frustrates us so much. . . . When you're by yourself it frustrates you a lot worse than when you're with a team."

A fifth-grade student points out that teaming not only helps with academic gaps but can also help close gaps in social skills.

> We're all at different academic levels, I've noticed, and [the teacher] does pair up the person who is kind of struggling with the person who is beyond what they need to be. . . . It does help because the person who is struggling, they're learning academically, but also the person who is beyond what they need to be—they're learning their socialization skills (Des Moines Public Schools, n.d.-b).

See Appendix A for more details on how academic teaming aligns to CASEL's SEL competencies, such as self-efficacy and stress management; see Appendix B for additional alignments to competencies from the Harvard study, such as empathy and perspective-taking and prosocial skills.

COMMITTING TO STUDENT-LED ACADEMIC TEAMING

Howe Elementary School educators say that after implementing academic teaming, they will never go back to teacher-centered classrooms. Principal Jill Burke cites undeniable student outcomes such as deep social-emotional learning, behavioral improvement, and higher academic achievement—in other words, higher SECL skills—as the reasons her teachers are convinced they are doing the right work, even if they were hesitant at the beginning of their journeys.

> Our teachers felt like what they were already doing was good—and it's not that it *wasn't* good. It just wasn't *good enough*. It wasn't getting the results that we truly needed to change our kids' lives. We needed to make a drastic shift to get better outcomes for *all* of our students, not the same kids that we're always getting better outcomes for. Once a few teachers started seeing results, that was the best way to get hesitant teachers to try teaming. You can't deny results like the achievement gaps narrowing or closing in certain grade levels and certain classrooms. The evidence is clear. Teachers had to feel it and see it, and once they realized that teaming is what was going to get better outcomes for kids, there was no turning back.

Julie Lake agrees that seeing her students access the rigorous educational experiences they deserve has made her job as a kindergarten teacher more joyful and meaningful.

> It can be a little stressful at first, but the outcome is worth all of that, and I'm not stressed anymore this year, because I've got my kids up and running and where they need to be. It's hard work, and I will tell anybody that, but it's the right work. Our data shows it. If you can do this right, the data will show that students are benefiting. I am a happier teacher because I'm not doing all the work. Yes, I'm planning it, but my students are doing the work, and so it's fun to see. I just love watching them grow and figure things out by themselves.

I just love watching them grow and figure things out by themselves.

NORTH HIGH SCHOOL

NORTH'S DEMOGRAPHICS

Student Population: 1,442
Number of Teachers: 68
Free and Reduced Price Lunch: 83%
Special Education: 21%
English Language Learners: 26%
White: 23%
Black: 28%
Hispanic: 31%
Asian: 11%
Two or More Races: 5%
Native Hawaiian or Pacific Islander: ,1%
American Indian/Alaska Native: ,1%

North High School is in its third year of implementation with Schools for Rigor. Ben Graeber was an administrator when North High School joined Schools for Rigor, and he is now in his second year leading the school as principal. Like Howe Elementary School, North is a Title I school—in fact, it is the only Title I high school in the Des Moines Public Schools District. Eighty-three percent of North students qualify for free and reduced price lunch. Graeber described how his students had usually coped with the challenges they faced: "The kids who had the most anxiety, stress, sadness, poverty, and trauma in their lives would go to the back of the classroom, put their hoods up, and be invisible." North teachers and staff were working hard to help students through their difficult circumstances, but not all students were engaging in their classroom work.

MOVING TO A CULTURE OF STUDENT EMPOWERMENT

Alyssa McDonald has been teaching for 13 years, and this is her seventh year at North High School. She has a split position between teaching English 4 and being an academic interventionist. According to McDonald, classroom instruction was very traditional at North. "It was very much the type of instruction that many of us grew up with: mostly focused on task completion, busy work, and textbook assignments, with limited discussion about learning."

In the 2016–17 school year, North joined Schools for Rigor, and teachers began to see how student-centered instruction was different from anything they had tried before. McDonald says, "The instruction has improved vastly from when I first came here. With academic teaming, teachers and students are more aware of exactly what they're learning and what it will look like once they've learned it."

Samantha Topps-Brown, a math teacher at North, is also seeing positive changes in her classroom. Topps-Brown has been a teacher for 10 years, and this is her third year at North. Topps-Brown found that academic teaming completely changed the way she thought about her role as a teacher:

> This work took everything that I knew about teaching, everything I've ever learned in teacher prep programs, and it really changed my perspective. I see a big shift from a lot of teacher responsibility and teacher ownership to student responsibility and student ownership. Now we have a classroom environment where students feel comfortable learning from each other, and my role is more of a coach or facilitator. I put the structures in place, but they're doing the work.

Principal Graeber is proud to report the positive culture shift at North High School due to this change in classroom instruction. He is pleased with how students perceive the changes since their school implemented academic teaming. Graeber says:

> Students talk about the transition in our school. Now they're tracking their own progress, and there are binders in every classroom that are full of learning targets and success criteria. There's so much information they've been provided access to that they didn't have before. They're now happy to say, "I cannot go into a classroom and be invisible. That's not who we are or what we're about." That's a culture change. Before, students were visitors to the learning. Now they're part of helping change our culture.

There's so much information they've been provided access to that they didn't have before. Before, students were visitors to the learning. Now they're part of helping change our culture.

North students are finding their voices through academic teaming. Their teachers note the benefits to students' self-confidence, self-efficacy, and growth mindset. McDonald teaches mostly moderate or low proficiency seniors in her English-4 class, since most high-proficiency students are in Advanced Placement English classes. McDonald says:

> The use of consistent tracking and clear targets and success criteria has helped students who believe they can't be good at English prove to themselves that not only can they be good at English, they can consistently be good at English and reach proficiency. That self-actualization process has been really good for my students, especially some students in subgroups who spent 11 years believing they could never be good at English and maybe were told that wasn't their strength. I think it's critical both for their own confidence, but also for their post-secondary success in job interviews, college, and trade schools. Kids need to be able to take their wonderful ideas and communicate them in a way that can be heard by a variety of different audiences. We're getting our kids ready to compete in a world we can't even imagine.

Kids need to be able to take their wonderful ideas and communicate them in a way that can be heard by a variety of different audiences. We're getting our kids ready to compete in a world we can't even imagine.

Graeber had previously observed teachers lecturing from the whiteboard for the entire 80-minute class period without giving students much opportunity for interaction. This was especially concerning for English language learners, who comprise 26% of the North student population and who may have been missing the opportunity to develop their oral language skills through traditional instruction. Graeber recalls an example of how academic teaming impacted English language learners at North.

> One of my ELL teachers in particular, if you go into her classroom, it's just so hopeful: these are students who have to learn the English language to survive, and with teaming they're learning in a style that's organic, natural, and humanizing. Their teacher makes sure she's only at the whiteboard for two or three minutes at a time. Then, she releases her students, and she's off interacting with them and tracking their learning. She has the freedom to adapt, to work with who she needs to work with. Her ability to have a classroom with flow is because of this work. She would not be the teacher she is without all of these strategies and all of this professional development around how to better serve these kids. If she can do it with students who don't know English very well, then my goodness, we can all do it.

It's just so hopeful: these are students who have to learn the English language to survive, and with teaming they're learning in a style that's organic, natural, and humanizing.

At North, all students are empowered to take an active part in their learning and build the critical social, emotional, and cognitive skills they'll need for life after high school.

CLASSROOM SYSTEMS FOR INCREASED STUDENT SUCCESS

Student empowerment, student ownership, and academic growth did not happen overnight at North High School. Teachers focused on creating strong systems for teaming in their classrooms in order for these outcomes to manifest. McDonald notes that these systems are what helped her utilize her "instructional tool bag" full of strategies. Once she put the team structures in place, McDonald used her instructional tool bag to increase her ability to track student learning and to make effective on-the-spot adaptations that best serve her students. McDonald says:

> *I can remediate on the fly to help fill in gaps for students. It's liberating for me as a teacher, and I think it's freeing for my students as well.*

Shifting away from set lesson plans filled me with a lot of trepidation at first. But once I had the systems in place for teaming, it was much easier for me to reach into my instructional tool bag and pull out a strategy. It makes me so much more effective in the moment and in situations that I couldn't have anticipated or planned for. I can remediate on the fly to help fill in gaps for students. It's liberating for me as a teacher, and I think it's freeing for my students as well.

As an academic interventionist, McDonald is also seeing impacts beyond her classroom. McDonald says there is much more proactive planning in PLCs due to the academic teaming methods—there is a greater emphasis on Tier I interventions to prevent students from getting to the point where they need more intensive interventions. She says:

> Intervention is happening in tiny chunks on a daily basis so that we don't have students quietly falling behind, digging themselves into a hole. We no longer have to figure out how to get 40 different kids out of 40 different holes two weeks into the learning process.

Mathematics teacher Topps-Brown found that the academic teaming systems are also allowing her to create conditions in her classroom where students self-regulate and problem-solve both academically and also socially and emotionally. After Topps-Brown put strong teaming structures into place, she stepped back, and students became more cognitively engaged as they worked through rigorous tasks without her help.

> *I remember one time I asked them, "Look, do you guys want me to just tell you how to find the answer?" And they said, "No! No, we will figure this out." That had never happened before in my eight years of teaching.*

I was so used to rescuing students before; sometimes I'd have 12 kids calling my name. It was overwhelming. Once students started working in teams, I realized that the more I take myself out of it, the more the kids become engaged and self-reliant through productive struggle. Students are checking each other's thinking, debating, finding consensus, and having aha! moments in their teams. I remember one time I asked them, "Look, do you guys want me to just tell you how to find the answer?" And they said, "No! No, we will figure this out." That had never happened before in my eight years of teaching at the time. It was amazing.

As much as academic teaming was a big shift for teachers, this new model of instruction was also a big shift for students. Topps-Brown says, "I've had kids that come from private schools and they'll say, 'Wow, this is different. My old teacher gave me a packet and we just did the work.'" Students at North are responding positively to academic teaming, even if it is very different from the way they used to learn. Topps-Brown recalls one student who joined her classroom in the middle of the semester and jumped right into teaming.

I introduced him to his team and told the other students to bring him on board. They immediately began to tell him, "Okay, so here's what we're doing. This is what we need to find, and this is what I've noticed and discovered, and now you can try this." It was incredible. He came into my class and got right on track with everybody from the first day. This kid went from the traditional style of teaching and learning to a team environment and right away he was able to collaborate, come up with solutions, ask questions, and understand learning targets and success criteria. It was just so seamless.

This kid went from the traditional style of teaching and learning to a team environment and right away he was able to collaborate, come up with solutions, ask questions, and understand learning targets and success criteria. It was just so seamless.

BETTER SERVING SPECIAL EDUCATION STUDENTS THROUGH TEAMS

North High School has a special education student population of 21 percent. In the 2015–16 school year, before North began implementing academic teaming through Schools for Rigor, graduation rates were 68.09 percent for special education students and 89.52 percent for general education students. It was more than a 20 percent gap.

After one year of implementation, special education student graduation rates rose to 84.51 percent, while the general education students' graduation rate held steady at 88.79 percent. Thus, the graduation gap between these two groups of students nearly closed in the 2016–17 school year (see Figure 4.3). Official data was not yet available for the following year (2017–18) at the time of this book's publication, but

When you're doing academic teaming with intentionality, each of those students is part of everything in the classroom; there's no division between them. It's definitely something to celebrate.

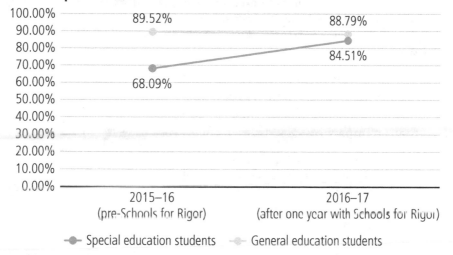

North High School Graduation Rates: Special Education and General Education Students

FIGURE 4.3. The gap in graduation rates between special education students and general education students nearly closed after one year of Schools for Rigor.

Graeber estimates the rates likely stayed about the same. He sees academic teaming as part of the reason for this striking improvement:

> We have a lot of classes that are "collabs" with general education and special education teachers working together with 15 general education students and 10 special education students. When you're doing academic teaming with intentionality, each of those students is part of everything in the classroom; there's no division between them. It's definitely something to celebrate.

NARROWING ACADEMIC AND SKILLS GAPS AT NORTH HIGH SCHOOL

As an academic interventionist, McDonald tracked data for 160 students in English 4, helping collect student evidence and measuring growth. McDonald says:

> Our students performed the single digits before—4–6% proficiency. Once we go through the teaching-learning-intervening process, we're getting proficiency numbers up to 40–50%. In an ideal world, those numbers would be 100%, but considering the number of challenges we face and the variety of skills that students come with, we're making progress. That is the best data I've seen in years.

Topps-Brown notices gaps narrowing between her mathematics class students as well, both in terms of grades and also students' skills.

> I have less students getting a "not met" or "progressing towards target," which in our district is a D or F grade. I have more kids successfully getting As and Bs, and

they're able to articulate what they can do. When I empowered students by teaching them how to properly use their resources to execute a big essential idea, that was huge. The achievement gaps for some of my kids with skills deficits started narrowing down.

Graeber is committed to continuing academic teaming and the Schools for Rigor work at North High School because of the transformative impact he sees.

I have teachers across subject areas—special education, ELL, math, science, English, vocal music—who are using academic teaming. Even if the Schools for Rigor partnership went away tomorrow, they would not stop one thing that they're doing. The student experience has been enhanced so much by this work, and we're seeing growth—proficiency scores are improving. That's exciting. This is the school we want to have.

> *When I empowered students by teaching them how to properly use their resources to execute a big essential idea, that was huge. The achievement gaps for some of my kids with skills deficits started narrowing down.*

> *This is the school we want to have.*

LINCOLN HIGH SCHOOL

LINCOLN'S DEMOGRAPHICS

Student Population: 2,359
Number of Teachers: 103
Free and Reduced Price Lunch: 75%
Special Education: 14%
English Language Learners: 14%
White: 47%
Black: 12%
Hispanic: 27%
Asian: 8%
Two or More Races: 5%
Native Hawaiian or Pacific Islander: ,1%
American Indian/Alaska Native: ,1%

Lincoln High School is in its second year of implementation with Schools for Rigor. Lincoln is a large school, serving 2,359 students spread across two campuses—the ninth-grade building is two miles down the road—and Principal Paul Williamson oversees both campuses and the challenges that come with them. Williamson is in his eighth year as principal at Lincoln; over the years, the student population has diversified greatly, and students come to school with increasingly complex needs, including 75 percent of students who qualify for free and reduced price lunch. Williamson says:

> Our community has changed drastically. When I got here, our student population was easily 75% white and only around 45% free and reduced [price] lunch. One of the big issues our kids now face is food security, so we started a food bank here a few years ago. We also have a lot of mobility in our student population. We embrace the diversity of our student population, but it also provides us with more challenges in the way that we think and the way that we teach.

With the progressively intensive needs of Lincoln High School students, it would be nearly impossible to have a truly meaningful impact on every student through traditional instruction.

POSITIVE CHANGES IN TEACHER PRACTICE

Lincoln joined Schools for Rigor in the 2017–18 school year. Although Williamson dealt with some resistance from teachers in the beginning, he now sees significant progress in their instructional practice, planning, and the effectiveness of their PLCs.

> A significant majority of our classrooms are now at least student-centered. We're not all on the team side of the matrix, like we want to be, but for the most part we've shifted away from traditional teacher-centered instruction. I'm seeing teachers plan more intentionally now than I've ever seen. Teachers are thinking about what student evidence they want to gather versus just doing their favorite activity. Before, too often activities were at the retrieval and comprehension levels; now we see more analysis-level tasks due to both our district's philosophy and the work with Schools for Rigor. This work has also allowed our PLCs to be more focused, with a greater emphasis on student data and more direction in our conversations about what's working or not working and how we are going to measure student learning.

Jean Mullen is in her fifth year of teaching at Lincoln. She teaches math for grades 9–12 and is conscious of the urgency around meeting the complex needs of her students. "I teach a very diverse population," she says. "So I really have to reach out to different student groups and make an instructional plan for how to reach them." This is Mullen's second year of implementing student-centered instruction; she can see a big difference between the way she taught before and how she teaches now, with teams, and how she is reaching more students:

It's a lot noisier in my classroom now, but if you take a closer listen, students are talking about mathematical content and using math language. It may seem a little hectic at first, but teaming has really transformed what my classroom looks like.

I've always had my students working in groups, but they were never in *teams*. Before, students sat near each other and were encouraged to work together and talk to each other, but I didn't have any of the supports to really help them be successful. Now I do have those supports in place and students know the expectations. I feel more prepared to teach my diverse student population; it's easier for me to notice when my students need interventions and when they don't, and to provide those interventions on the spot. As far as the classroom culture and productivity, it's a lot noisier in my classroom now, but if you take a closer listen, students are talking about mathematical content and using math language. It may seem a little hectic at first, but teaming has really transformed what my classroom looks like.

GROWTH IN STUDENT ACHIEVEMENT, ENGAGEMENT, OWNERSHIP, AND LEADERSHIP

The changes in teacher practice at Lincoln are leading to promising student outcomes as far as equity and access is concerned. Williamson is seeing greater engagement and ownership among different subgroups.

> I think equity can come through academic teaming. Kids that would often disengage are now not disengaging nearly as much. Our special education students, ELL students, and all of our different racial and ethnic groups—they're not disengaging from conversations. Kids are in groups and doing the heavy lifting often, and success criteria has been huge for helping our students know what's expected of them.

Our special education students, ELL students, and all of our different racial and ethnic groups— they're not disengaging from conversations. Kids are in groups and doing the heavy lifting often.

Mullen agrees that students are showing increased self-motivation and are setting more challenging academic goals for themselves. They're also building peer support networks and pushing each other toward success.

> In previous years, students were fairly comfortable just settling for where they were. A lot more of my students are pushing for the A now. The team environment has really helped students take ownership of their learning and push themselves for higher achievement. They're advocating for their own learning, and I don't have to motivate them as much. They motivate each other.

Mullen recalls one student in particular whose self-confidence skyrocketed as he became a leader in her classroom and began engaging with his peers.

> When I first met this student, his mom said he tends to feel socially awkward and struggles interacting with other students, so I kept that information on my radar. Through the course of the year, especially towards the second semester, this student was a definite leader in my classroom. I would verify his work and without me even prompting him he'd ask, "Can I go around and help others?" So I said, "Absolutely, yes." It was really cool for me to see how much he transformed as a person and how he took on a leadership role.

Lincoln High School is seeing gains academically, as well. They made improvements on their state MAP® Growth™ assessment scores from Spring 2017 to Spring 2018, after only a few months of implementing Schools for Rigor. The percent of students meeting growth in mathematics rose by

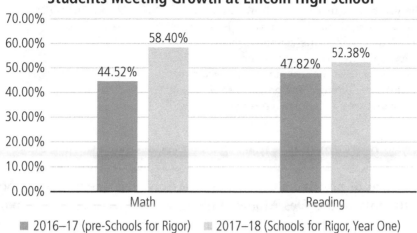

FIGURE 4.4. The percent of students meeting growth at Lincoln High School rose in both mathematics and reading after less than one year of Schools for Rigor.

13.88 percent, and the percent of students meeting growth in reading rose by 4.56 percent (see Figure 4.4).

CONTINUING TOWARD A BRIGHTER FUTURE

Teachers are saying, "Now that I've taught this way I don't think I could ever go back. I can't believe I even taught the way I did five years ago."

Although many teachers at Lincoln High School may have been reluctant when they first partnered with Schools for Rigor and started implementation a year and a half ago, Williamson is gradually seeing more buy-in. He says, "The work is challenging, but it's getting better. Teachers are saying, 'Now that I've taught this way I don't think I could ever go back. I can't believe I even taught the way I did five years ago.'"

Mullen is one of these teachers. She is committed to continue using academic teaming structures in her classroom because of the positive changes she sees.

It's been a learning experience for me and my colleagues and my students, but we're going to keep with it because the outcomes are great. It just takes time. But once you really dive in and you see the results and students see results, you'll want to keep using these classroom structures. I would not ever backtrack. I want to keep growing.

Williamson is hopeful for a schoolwide transformation as Lincoln evolves toward academic teaming as the norm in every classroom.

Second-order change takes time, but this is the right work. Every time we do buildingwide walkthroughs and look for key indicators we are seeing growth in just about every area. We're not where we want to be yet, but we're showing growth. I see more students engaged than I ever have. Kids are doing more of the work in the classroom and teachers are putting more work into intentional planning. I fully believe that the techniques and structures we're learning through this process are changing the way that we do school in a positive way.

> *The techniques and structures we're learning through this process are changing the way that we do school in a positive way.*

REMARKABLE ACHIEVEMENT RESULTS IN DES MOINES

The evidence of positive student impact is not just anecdotal. Schools for Rigor students in the Des Moines Public Schools district saw remarkable gains in academic achievement. In order to analyze these gains, Schools for Rigor students were matched to like students in the district whose schools were not participating in Schools for Rigor and who had similar Fall pretest scores on Northwest Evaluation Association (NWEA) assessments. A What Works Clearinghouse certified reviewer assessed the effectiveness of Schools for Rigor, ensuring results met What Works Clearinghouse Design Standards with Reservations, and only statistically significant findings are included below. Sample sizes (*n*) in the figures only include Schools for Rigor students; however, all Schools for Rigor students were matched to the same number of control students to estimate the program's impact.

> Learning Gains: "The notion of **learning gain** is a deceptively simple one. We can define it as the improvement in a student's **learning** between the beginning and end of a course." (Galloway & Lancaster, n.d.)

In the 2017–18 school year, there were 10,431 total students in 22 participating Schools for Rigor in Des Moines out of 64 total schools in the district. Students at all Schools for Rigor experienced a statistically significant impact. Schools for Rigor students had a 7 percent improvement in reading and a 3 percent improvement in mathematics over the gain otherwise expected within 162 school days. This improvement translates into the equivalent of receiving an additional 11 days of learning in reading and an additional 6 days in mathematics for Schools for Rigor students. In other words, all students in the district would require an additional 11 days of reading instruction and an additional 6 days of mathematics instruction to

---

[1]The **What Works Clearinghouse** (**WWC**) provides educators, policy makers, researchers, and the public with a central source of scientific evidence on **what works** in education to improve student outcomes. Its goal is to help decision makers contend with differing messages from research studies and product offerings. (https://ies.ed.gov/ncee/wwc/WhatWeDo)

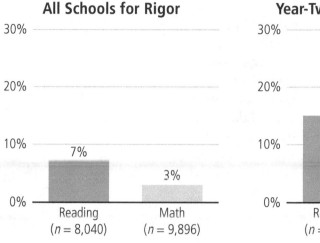

FIGURE 4.5. Gains in reading and mathematics for all Schools for Rigor students in Des Moines in the 2017–2018 school year.

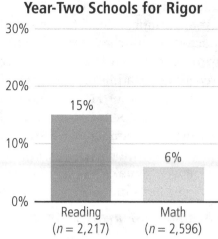

FIGURE 4.6. Gains in reading and mathematics for Schools for Rigor Year Two students in Des Moines in the 2017–2018 school year.

make the same learning gains Schools for Rigor students did with academic teaming (see Figure 4.5).

Schools for Rigor students made gains equivalent to an additional 21 days of learning in reading and an additional 10 days in mathematics in the second year of implementation.

Schools for Rigor students in the six schools that had been implementing academic teaming for a full two years had even more impressive gains. These students had a 15 percent improvement in reading and a 6 percent improvement in mathematics over the gain otherwise expected within 162 school days. This improvement translates into the equivalent of receiving an additional 21 days of learning in reading and an additional 10 days of learning in mathematics for Year Two Schools for Rigor students. Simply put, all students in the district would require an additional 10 days of mathematics instruction and an additional 21 days of reading instruction to make the same learning gains Year Two Schools for Rigor students did with academic teaming (see Figure 4.6). Year Two Schools for Rigor had the benefit of having a Learning Sciences International Leadership Coach directly coach the principal and leadership teams at these schools. In addition, students had the benefit of having teachers with more experience implementing the techniques.

In its second year of implementing Schools for Rigor, Howe Elementary School had a statistically significant improvement in mathematics. Howe students had a 35 percent improvement in mathematics over the gain otherwise expected in matched control students. This improvement translates into the equivalent of receiving an additional 35 days of learning in mathematics for Howe Schools for Rigor students over a period of 162 school days. In other words, all students in the district would require an additional 35 days of mathematics instruction to make the same learning gains Howe students did with academic teaming.

Howe Elementary Schools for Rigor students made gains equivalent to an additional 35 days of learning in mathematics.

Schools for Rigor students at the two high schools in this research study had the largest learning gains. Lincoln High School (a Year One school) and North High School (a Year Two school) implemented

High school students in Schools for Rigor made gains equivalent to an additional 61 days of learning in reading and an additional 42 days in mathematics.

academic teaming as part of Schools for Rigor. Schools for Rigor high school students had a 37 percent improvement in reading and a 26 percent improvement in mathematics over the gains otherwise expected within 162 school days. This improvement translates into an additional 61 days of learning in reading and an additional 42 days in mathematics for Schools for Rigor students. That is to say, all students in the district would require an additional 61 days of reading instruction and an additional 42 days of mathematics instruction to make the same learning gains that high school Schools for Rigor students did with academic teaming (see Figure 4.7).

Des Moines Public School's implementation of Learning Sciences Schools for Rigor made quite a bit of progress in closing their achievement gaps. Black students in Schools for Rigor reduced the black–white achievement gap by 7 percent in reading and 6 percent in mathematics within 162 school days. Schools for Rigor students with disabilities (SWD) reduced the SWD–non-SWD achievement gap by 6 percent in reading and 5 percent in

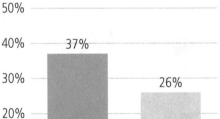

Schools for Rigor High Schools

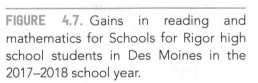

FIGURE 4.7. Gains in reading and mathematics for Schools for Rigor high school students in Des Moines in the 2017–2018 school year.

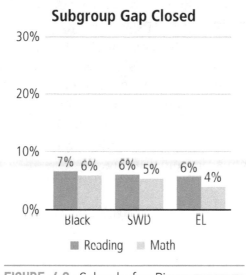

Subgroup Gap Closed

FIGURE 4.8. Schools for Rigor progress in narrowing achievement gaps in Des Moines in the 2017–2018 school year.

mathematics. Schools for Rigor English learners (EL) reduced the EL–Non-EL achievement gap by 6 percent in reading and 4 percent in mathematics (see Figure 4.8).

MAJOR SUCCESSES IN DES MOINES PUBLIC SCHOOLS

- ❖ Howe Elementary School reports closing the achievement gap in kindergarten and first-grade classrooms.
- ❖ North High School reports closing the graduation rate gap between special education and general education students.
- ❖ Howe students had a 35 percent improvement in mathematics over the gain otherwise expected.
- ❖ North and Lincoln students had a 37 percent improvement in reading and a 26 percent improvement in mathematics over the gains otherwise expected.
- ❖ Schools for Rigor narrowed achievement gaps in the Des Moines district for various subgroups by 4–7 percent.
- ❖ Year Two Schools for Rigor had a 15 percent improvement in reading and a 6 percent improvement in mathematics over the gain otherwise expected. Across all 22 Schools for Rigor, students showed a 7 percent

improvement in reading and a 3 percent improvement in mathematics over the gain otherwise expected.

❖ Des Moines Public School district teachers, principals, district administrators, and students themselves recognized the immense academic, behavioral, and social and emotional growth due to participating in academic teaming as part of Schools for Rigor.

❖ Classroom evidence showed that all students—including English language learners, special education students, and black students—benefited from academic teaming.

📄 **POINTS TO CONSIDER: CHAPTER 4**

This page is to jot down points from Chapter 4 to consider later and discuss with colleagues and students.

⤳ WHAT'S COMING

In Chapter 5, we explain how school and district leaders can lead the change to academic teaming. We include guidance on how to create and communicate a compelling vision, how to reinforce high expectations, and how to support teachers who may feel enthusiastic, hesitant, or even resistant. We examine the importance of systems such as instructional rounds and communities of practice and common pitfalls to avoid. We also share insights and advice from educators who have led the shift to academic teaming in their schools and districts.

CHAPTER 5:

LEADING CLASSROOM CHANGE TO ACADEMIC TEAMING

In every school, there will always be some brave teachers who are up for the challenge to implement academic teams and to stick with it until the benefits emerge for both students and teachers. But what about teachers who may be more hesitant? Every school will inevitably have some teachers who are not as quick to dive in. To achieve true second-order change, we must ask teachers to change core instructional practices that they feel comfortable with and may feel are working for them. Teachers may need to leave their comfort zones to try other practices that could truly transform their classrooms.

To achieve true second-order change, we must ask teachers to change core instructional practices that they feel comfortable with and may feel are working for them. Teachers may need to leave their comfort zones to try other practices that could truly transform their classrooms.

Simply stated, first-order change occurs when we tweak or update our mental model of core instruction: for example, by asking teachers to add more student engagement into their lectures. The basic relationship between teacher and student remains unchanged. Second-order change happens when we challenge our entire mental model of teaching with significantly revised roles for the teacher and student. For teachers to shift their mental model of core instruction, they need to change *both* their vision for classroom instruction and their habits of teaching.

But we are not simply asking teachers to change for the sake of changing. Associate Superintendent Matt Smith talks about the heart of his vision for transforming instruction in his district:

> The vision of instruction can't exist in isolation from social and emotional learning and equity and access. All of these educational goals are interconnected, and educators need to be able to see that. Otherwise, folks can lose their purpose of why we come to work every day, which is to create equity and access and opportunities for students and staff. The multifaceted approach of academic teaming offers children not just an instructionally sound research-based model; it also supports the belongingness and connectedness of students with one another and with their teachers. It offers students the opportunity to build compassion and empathy, and it also builds 21st-century skills around how to collaborate with team members. And so when you wrap all of

those outcomes into the vision of why we're doing what we're doing, I think that's what folks can connect to. We have the head, the heart, and the hand of our work: We have the research and science, which is the head; the social-emotional learning and equity, which is the heart; and the voice of teachers and students leading their own learning, which is the hand. When you bring all of these components—the whole spirit of the person—into education, that's where we see small miracles each and every day around closing gaps for students.

In implementing academic teaming in schools across the country, it has been our experience at Learning Sciences International that schoolwide adoption in every classroom does not occur without sustained support from district leaders, the principal, and a strong school leadership team, including teacher leaders. This final chapter provides the leadership pathway to full school adoption that empowers teachers and their students to make remarkable gains in social, emotional, and cognitive learning through effective student-led academic teams.

Below, we examine the leadership best practices identified by Learning Sciences Applied Research Center, where we have taken hundreds of schools successfully through the academic teaming professional development and coaching process.

> *We have the head, the heart, and the hand of our work: We have the research and science, which is the head; the social-emotional learning and equity, which is the heart; and the voice of teachers and students leading their own learning, which is the hand. When you bring all of these components—the whole spirit of the person—into education, that's where we see small miracles each and every day around closing gaps for students.*

LEADING THE CHANGE IN VISION

One of the most important responsibilities for the principal and school leadership team is to establish a clear vision for core instruction and to communicate a compelling purpose for why this change of instruction is necessary and urgent. In *Who Moved My Standards?* (Toth, 2016), a parable illustrates the case for deep instructional shifts by contrasting how much the world has changed while our traditional teaching has not kept pace and is not equipping students with the skills they need to thrive in the new economy. The Old Economy Classroom Environment versus New Economy Classroom Environment chart in Table 5.1 shows how a transformation in core instruction, from traditional pedagogy to academic teams, benefits both teachers and students. As we touched on in the Introduction chapter, students urgently need these skills to compete in a global high-tech marketplace. Refer to Appendix H for a detailed comparison between Old Economy

TABLE 5.1. The differences between an Old Economy Classroom Environment and a New Economy Classroom Environment (Adapted from Toth, 2016, p. 46)

Old Economy Classroom Environment	New Economy Classroom Environment
Teacher is doing most of the work.	Students are doing most of the work.
Teacher is doing most of the talking and directing.	Students are doing most of the talking and are directing their own work.
Teacher feels like he or she is pushing the students to learn.	Students take ownership of their academic progress and pull toward their learning goals.
Students have a hard time visualizing how the learning will help them in the real world.	Students are seeing the connections to the real world through their work.
Teacher feels the pressure to engage and hold students' attention.	Students are highly engaged in complex tasks and real-world problems.
Teacher feels fatigue and the pressure to cover content.	Students are feeling mentally stretched but excited about the task and what they are discovering.

classroom activities and New Economy classroom activities aligned with Bloom's Taxonomy.

Many schools are already deeply engaged in social and emotional learning (SEL) or growth mindset initiatives. These initiatives, for example, can provide a rationale for the second-order change needed to implement teaming because student-led academic teaming helps embed these worthy goals (empathy, grit, constructive argument, etc.) into classroom core instruction. Academic teaming provides concrete, practical opportunities for students to practice SECL skills, rather than merely learning them in the abstract.

Academic teaming provides concrete, practical opportunities for students to practice SECL skills, rather than merely learning them in the abstract.

For schools that serve high populations of children in poverty, one of the most compelling reasons to pursue the second-order change to academic teaming is because these New Economy and SECL skills can help equip students with the life skills needed to succeed economically after school. The skills they learn with teaming have the potential to help lift graduates

---

CONNECTING EDUCATORS TO THE VISION

Walnut Middle School Assistant Principal Selena Wardyn remarks:

"I really believe, as a leader, in empowering your team. We didn't say, *Here's our vision, believe in it.* It was *Let's talk about what our vision should be at Walnut Middle School.* We worked through ideas like New Economy versus Old Economy skills and what the future will hold for our students, and we arrived at our vision together. Second-order change doesn't happen if you don't have people that believe in it.

What I see now is focus and energy that wasn't there before. Our teachers have pride in what they're doing and what they're accomplishing. They want people to come in and see the exciting things they're doing because they're really proud of their kids and they're proud of the work they're doing."

> *What I see now is focus and energy that wasn't there before. Our teachers have pride in what they're doing and what they're accomplishing.*

---

out of the cycle of poverty. Any of these advantages can be communicated to stakeholders as compelling and urgent reasons for transforming our classroom practices to academic teaming. The rationale for a school's transformation must be *compelling* to the school's leadership and teachers (as well as the larger community and school board).

CONSTANTLY COMMUNICATING THE VISION

Establishing the vision and compelling purpose for changing core instruction to academic teaming may be the easy part. It is the relentless and necessary follow-through in communication, action, and accountability that cements the understanding that this initiative is real, it is not going away, and school leaders expect that everyone will eventually get on board. As we commonly hear in the business world, "When you are tired of saying it, they are just starting to hear it." School leaders will do well to leverage the school year theme and every communications platform to rally the school around the vision for core instruction. The vision must be grounded in compelling student-centered reasons if it is to be implemented with purpose. Teachers understandably will want to hear from other teachers and students who have gone through the process. For examples of students and teachers discussing the change process, see the videos of schools and classrooms transformed by academic teaming on the companion website, www.AcademicTeaming.com.

IDENTIFYING EARLY ADOPTERS

A common error many school leaders make is to try to co-opt the resisters in the faculty at the start. This essentially gives the power of veto to a few. Instead, we advise school leaders to leave resisters largely alone and focus energy and support on the early adopters; this group of teachers is the *coalition of the willing*. These teachers identify with the vision for core instruction, and the compelling purpose for change resonates with them. They are the risk-takers who will try out teaming techniques in their classrooms and persist until they get results with students, while sharing what worked and what is not yet working.

The school leaders we work with report that teachers say, time and again, "I didn't know my kids could do that." It is amazing how quickly students will respond to increased ownership and engagement in academic teams.

Teaching is often an incredibly isolated act in classrooms, so it is important to bring the coalition of the willing together regularly into a community of practice where teachers can excitedly share small wins on what is working and how it could work even better. School leaders and coaches should celebrate each small win with the team, encouraging others to take more instructional risks. The school leaders we work with report that teachers say, time and again, "I didn't know my kids could do that." It is amazing how

---

NURTURING TRUE SECOND—ORDER CHANGE

I think the power was in the teachers seeing one another implement teaming and not forcing teaming on them. It wasn't compliance. It was second-order change.

"Our early adopters rose to the top right away, with their energy and excitement and desire to get involved. So, of course, that's who we started with. For me, as a leader, it was the first time I was focusing my energy on people who were really on board. Everybody came on at their own time. One of our seventh-grade teachers sat down at my desk one day and said, 'Okay, I get it now. I wasn't sure; I wasn't on board, but now I see it's working.' I think the power was in the teachers seeing one another implement teaming and not forcing teaming on them. It wasn't compliance. It was second-order change."

—*Selena Wardyn, Assistant Principal of Walnut Middle School, Grand Island Public Schools, Nebraska*

quickly students will respond to increased ownership and engagement in academic teams. If a school has instructional coaches, they should be co-leading the process to support teachers in the academic teaming implementation and in identifying early successes to share with the school leadership team.

EXPANDING THE COALITION

Once school leaders see early adopter classrooms showing evidence of increased student voice, participation, and engagement, they should ask other teachers to come in and observe. The goal is not to wait until the early adopters are perfect in their implementation. Once their confidence is building, school leaders can invite teachers who are not participating but who are curious and open to seeing how teachers and students are successfully handling the shift to academic teaming. These instructional rounds are easy to get started. Below are the essentials for effective instructional rounds to expand the coalition of the willing:

1. Identify an implementing classroom with emerging visible and auditory *student* evidences, where students talk and process more about content with increased engagement. Ask if the teacher would be willing to allow peers in to see how the students are doing.

2. Identify a few teachers open to the concept who will visit the classroom during a scheduled time agreeable to the visiting and host teachers. Provide release time coverage of the visiting teachers' classrooms. This can be accomplished with a floating substitute teacher, with coverage by an administrator or specialists, or by briefly putting two classrooms together.

3. Ensure that the principal or a coach can accompany visiting teachers to focus observers on the meaningful aspects of academic teaming that they should look for in classrooms, such as students discussing and learning together.

4. Make clear that the visiting teacher is *not* observing the host teacher to provide feedback unless the host teacher requests it. Instead, the visiting teacher should identify what the host teacher and students are doing differently from practices and activities in the visiting teacher's own classroom.

5. Be sure that the visiting teachers have time to debrief with the accompanying principal or coach. Teachers can reflect on the classroom evidences compared to their own classrooms and join in the implementation process, which will add other teachers to the growing number of teachers who are implementing.

THE AHA! OF INSTRUCTIONAL ROUNDS

Just let teachers go into each other's classrooms and see academic teaming in action. That is going to be more convincing than if you try to strong-arm them. Once teachers see how well teaming works, they will naturally want to try it themselves.

"On the Learning Sciences' Coaching for Implementation professional development days, teachers started visiting each other's classrooms, and afterward some teachers started observing each other during their planning time. Teachers had their biggest aha! moments during these instructional rounds. For example, one teacher had a lot of really quiet and not very confident students in her classroom. This teacher added a teaming structure called 'talking chips' to encourage students who were apprehensive about talking. All the students got involved and held each other accountable. During instructional rounds, other teachers saw this teacher using the talking chips, so now those teachers are using talking chips, too. Our advice would be: do not force implementation. Just let teachers go into each other's classrooms and see academic teaming in action. That is going to be more convincing than if you try to strong-arm them. Once teachers see how well teaming works, they will naturally want to try it themselves."

—*Sheree Stockwell, Principal at Jefferson Elementary School, Grand Island Public Schools, Nebraska*

One important caution is worth mentioning here: the principal must ensure that early adopters do not form a clique that is separated from the rest of the faculty. As observing teachers partner with observed teachers, they create a second tier of implementing teachers and further spread the message. The goal is to get early classroom evidences and celebrate those evidences to expand the coalition bit by bit until the whole school is implementing. When 30–40 percent of teachers are implementing with strong student evidences, the school will be nearing the tipping point. There will be more peer pressure to participate than to not participate. Once that happens, most schools have the momentum to permanently change the culture of classrooms.

The reality is that teachers, like most people, can be risk adverse. They may hold back from being the first to try something new just because the principal thinks it might be a good idea. Some teachers will wait to see if the new initiative and support are going to persist. Once these well-meaning teachers see that the leadership team is serious and supportive, and early adopting teachers who took the risks are reaping benefits in their classrooms, they become much more comfortable in joining the implementation.

ALIGNING THE SUPPORT SYSTEMS

As the coalition of willing teachers grows, school leaders will want to help the coalition move quickly from an ad hoc community of practice to more formal systems of support. One of these systems of support can be peer learning, where an early adopter picks a second teacher—probably a mid-adopter who is willing to learn but a little slow to get going—to pair up with. They plan together and visit each other to learn, process, and take risks together.

Turning teacher meetings (or better yet, professional learning communities, or PLCs) into communities of practice for academic teaming is one of the best ways to create additional systems of support. Teacher meetings will give teachers a designated time to plan team tasks for their lessons and to share best practices, thereby helping struggling teachers troubleshoot their classroom implementation.

CONSISTENT PLCS YIELD STRONG ACADEMIC IMPROVEMENT

"Our third-grade PLC was the most consistent about implementing academic teaming. They worked on success criteria and learning targets and developed plans together. They really bought into their process. When I look at the student test scores, that grade level has shown the most improvement throughout the year in comparison to other grade levels."
—*Michael Persampieri, Assistant Principal at Starr Elementary School, Grand Island Public Schools, Nebraska*

Aligning instructional coaching, instructional rounds, and professional learning communities to achieve the vision for core instruction is a way to magnify the implementation effects. Even with these on track, there is absolutely no substitute for the principal setting a schedule of weekly classroom visits to inspect and celebrate the implementation of academic teaming. Classroom visits must be approached from a growth perspective. Everyone in the system is learning and growing together. During the classroom visits, the principal and leadership team grow alongside the teachers with whom they share feedback. This unyielding inspection and subsequent feedback regarding the vision for core instruction sets the tone for the entire school culture. It is the best signal to teachers that academic teaming is not a flavor-of-the-month initiative, and that it is here to stay.

Classroom visits must be approached from a growth perspective. Everyone in the system is learning and growing together.

Principals will have to be consistent and *persistent* in their classroom visits. They will eventually need to focus on ways to bring academic teaming to the remaining nonimplementing classrooms. By being in classrooms and seeing firsthand the degree of implementation, the principal is equipped to guide the school leadership team to its transformative vision for core instruction.

Another way to magnify implementation effects is to communicate schoolwide trends weekly to the entire faculty and students. At Walnut Middle School, Principal Rod Foley handled this communication masterfully with public displays of weekly data. Both the faculty and students knew what teachers were working on in each classroom. Students became part of the culture of change as they asked teachers who were not implementing when they would get to work in teams in their classrooms.

RESISTANCE WANES

Principals report that it is often in the second year of implementation when their schools reach the tipping point for broad-based implementation and when the majority of classroom teachers adopt academic teaming. In Year Two, several factors are generally in place: a significant number of teachers are advocates, after having first-year success; the coaching and PLC systems are aligned; and the principal and school leadership team are more comfortable with the first-year learning. Leaders may now increase their leadership and support for student-led academic teaming, and most of the more reluctant teachers should be willing to attempt teaming in their classrooms.

Given that implementing new instructional practices is inherently risky for teachers, we advise school leaders to separate the academic teaming implementation from the demands of the teacher evaluation process. It is important that teachers feel safe to take risks even before they are good at teaming techniques. Once they get comfortable and fluent with increased student evidences of academic teaming, it is appropriate to honor teachers with positive evaluation comments.

Now we come to the question of how school leaders should handle the small number of hard-core resisters who want to close their doors and continue teaching the way they always have. In our experience, most of these resisters do convert over time as the school culture changes. Students may even begin to ask why they cannot work in academic teams as they do in other classrooms. A few teacher holdouts may leave of their own volition. On rare occasions, principals may counsel reluctant teachers to move to other schools where academic teaming is not a focus. Though there may be a few persistent resisters who require additional strategies to bring them into the new school culture, we hear many more stories where teachers nearing retirement and feeling burnt out have become re-energized by their students and extended their classroom careers, thanks to academic teaming.

CENTRAL OFFICE SUPPORT

Most of academic teaming implementation work is with our Schools for Rigor initiative through the Learning Sciences Applied Research Center and the Ignite Student Academic Teaming professional development and coaching series. Our implementation work takes place most often at the school level; however, we have a growing number of districts that are implementing student-led academic teaming districtwide. The implementation process is similar to school-level implementation, but it differs in some notable ways:

1. **Vision for core instruction and classroom culture**—Just as principals need to do at the school level, superintendents need to ask questions of the whole district to set a vision for core instruction and classroom culture. A superintendent may ask, "In our district, how do we want students to experience core instruction and classroom culture? Do we want to develop the whole child, including SECL and preparation for success in the New Economy? Do we want to increase equity and access for all children as learners in every classroom?" These goals need to be crafted into the district's strategic plan so that student-led academic teaming becomes the core instruction and catalyzes the shift to New Economy skills, social-emotional learning, and equity in every classroom. (See the Appendices for more detailed information on how academic teaming aligns with SEL competencies, New Economy skills, equity, and more.)

2. **Communication with stakeholders, including the board and community**—When districts begin this process, it is helpful to frame the discussion with two central questions: "Has the world changed since you were a student? If so, then how should education change from what you experienced as a student?"

   These questions spur thoughtful discussions around the need to shift instruction to prepare students differently for the future economy. Once the key stakeholders have bought in to the need for change, the superintendent (or cabinet-level designee) ensures that all district messaging reinforces the new vision, the need for change, and how the implementation plan will benefit teachers, students, and the community. Once student-led academic teaming implementation has begun, the superintendent should regularly report progress toward the vision goals to all stakeholders.

3. **Coalition of the willing among schools**—It is typically best if a few schools are selected to start the process. In the Grand Island, Nebraska, public school district, for example, superintendent Tawana Grover chose just three schools to implement student-led academic teaming in Year One as Schools for Rigor. These three schools became lab schools in the district and eventually served to model the pathway for other schools. All the schools in the district were encouraged to visit the three lab schools during the year to see the transformative process of student-led academic teaming in action. Selecting a few demonstration schools for first-year implementation is a key foundational concept of the Schools for Rigor initiative, and it works amazingly well. (See www.LearningSciences.com/rigor for case studies and research reports.)

    These schools are selected because central office administrators believe their principals can successfully win over faculty and implement student-led academic teaming in core instruction schoolwide. The school leaders are early adopters: capable leaders who are *instructionally strong* and willing to take risks. They believe in the vision and commit to leading, even if it means making some of their faculty uncomfortable for a while until they work through it. This last requirement—a willingness to continue the work despite some pushback—is crucial.

4. **Principal rounds**—Once these demonstration schools start producing student evidences through academic teaming, the district can invite other principals to visit the implementing classrooms and learn from the process, thus building the coalition of the willing among school leaders. Districts can identify principals most open to the concept and start with them. These visits typically are limited to four or five participants who meet briefly with demonstration school leaders to learn about student-led academic teaming, to learn how the implementation is progressing, and to preview what principals should look for when they visit these classrooms.

    This brief orientation is necessary because unskilled observers tend to look at how the classroom is managed or if students are noisy. School leaders must focus participants on the most important aspects of a learning culture involving teaming. In classrooms implementing student-led academic teaming, visitors should concentrate on evidence of student ownership, self-regulation, engagement, energy, and the level of content discussions the students are having in their teams.

    After two or three classroom visits, the group should pause to talk about the students and the trends they have seen. These visits become an opportunity to teach nonimplementing principals to see instruction differently. At the end of the visit, the group debriefs to let the visiting principals reflect on what they saw. How are the classrooms they observed different from those in their own schools?

5. **Principals' community of practice**—Districts should form a community of practice among the implementing principals with quality time for them to openly share implementation strategies, to share successes, and to support each other on implementation struggles. This is a critical and often missing element of change leadership. In addition to a community of practice for these early adopting principals, in the district's regular principal meetings, early adopters can share wins about how their classrooms are changing. This becomes the primary platform, along with principal rounds, for gaining momentum for the student-led academic teaming initiative among school leaders.

6. **Inspection by principal supervisors**—Individuals who supervise the principals should also attend student-led academic teaming trainings to learn how to support the implementing principals. The principal supervisor should take on the role of co-learner and model the collaborative relationship of the work. Principal supervisors will need to learn how to conduct academic teaming school walks and provide feedback and celebrations for each school's incremental wins on their journey to a new core instruction. Given the risks of changing one's school, and the lack of consequences for playing it safe, pressure and support from the principal supervisors will help spread academic teaming in core instruction among schools. Principal supervisor training and coaching is essential in any districtwide implementation.

7. **Superintendent inspection visits to schools and classrooms to celebrate wins**—Nothing makes a statement like superintendent visits to highlight schools that are implementing student-led academic teaming well. Such visits encourage schools to do more. On the other hand, when superintendents visit schools that are not making progress, it reinforces expectations. The superintendent can send the strongest possible signal by visiting schools and inspecting for the changes in classrooms and by holding district teams and principal supervisors accountable for supporting schools in their transformation. Most important, the superintendent should celebrate and showcase the schools, teachers, and students that implement well, including sharing these successes with the community through the district's social media accounts.

In Grand Island, Nebraska, for instance, Superintendent Dr. Tawana Grover schedules and protects time each week to visit schools. These three-and-a-half hour "Thursday Walks" are the first thing scheduled on her calendar each year. As Dr. Grover says, "Even the community knows these times are sacred for the superintendent and the executive cabinet." Each visit concludes with a debriefing and allows the superintendent to celebrate and reinforce milestones.

PITFALLS TO AVOID

Struggles are common when we ask teachers to implement new strategies, especially something as transformative as student-led academic teaming, but school and district leaders can prepare themselves in advance to minimize the effects of these struggles.

1. **Dispel misconceptions**—Despite best attempts, misconceptions will arise, and leaders will have to combat them for a while with correct information and constant communication. For example, one misconception that seems to reoccur is the incorrect perception that teachers are no longer allowed to "teach" or "talk to students." The school leader will need to explain that lecture and direct instruction play an important role in learning, but for specific and limited periods. Direct instruction becomes a launchpad for team tasks that allow students to talk about and engage with content. Just as 100 percent lecture is not conducive to deep learning, we are not looking for 100 percent academic teaming either. There needs to be a weighted balance that allows students to receive the benefits of both direct instruction and academic teaming, as we have discussed in Chapter 1.

2. **Helping teachers let go**—The most common error in classrooms is that the teacher holds back from releasing responsibility and autonomy to students. Students will produce evidences of learning proportional to the amount of autonomy given to them. If the teacher keeps rescuing students and not allowing for productive struggle in academic teams, students will not realize the full benefits. Often teachers need another set of eyes from a coach, peer, or administrator to see this issue. Coaches and peers can encourage the teacher to take a step back and let the students discuss and shine. Remind teachers that the brain that does the work is the brain that learns. Research studies continue to show that when students freely discuss what they are learning *while* they are learning it, they gain a deeper understanding of the learning and are more likely to retain it (e.g., Murphy et al., 2018).

Sometimes teachers tell us they do not know what to do if they release this much to students. They need support and encouragement to understand there is still plenty for the teacher to do. The teacher's role has shifted from information-giver and rescuer to a facilitator who is closely tracking the learning to make efficient and effective decisions in the classroom. When teachers do step back, they are usually amazed at what students are capable of learning, remembering, and doing.

3. **Leadership courage**—Second-order change is uncomfortable by definition because it requires teachers to modify their role in the teaching–learning process. As this discomfort manifests, leaders have a choice—they can either back down from the demand or lead through it until teachers see the evidences of learning in their classrooms.

   We have seen leaders do both, with predictable results. Principals who smartly lead through discomfort have more successful implementations than those who back off and circle around to it again. To be clear, the principal must always listen to teacher feedback for important issues—and there will be issues. A successful leader must be able to resolve real issues while maintaining the pressure for change. Leaders need this combination of pressure and support to effect real transformation.

4. **Identifying priorities**—One of the least effective ways to lead second-order change is to have multiple *competing* priorities at the same time. Allowing priorities to equally compete removes the power of focus. Of course, there will always be multiple priorities, but the role of leadership is to provide focus and relentless follow-through on the main priority. The school leader ensures that other priorities are aligned, rather than competing.

   Once this is determined, the school leader makes sure to communicate clearly to faculty and staff how other priorities support the main focus. A school leader should consider setting weekly and monthly goals for the implementation and hold daily 10-minute standups with the school leadership team to ensure focus and review what actions are being taken to achieve weekly goals. It is very helpful to report weekly and monthly to the entire school the percent of progress toward goals. Change is hard work. Daily focus and setting weekly goals are necessary to make change happen successfully.

   A long-term commitment is just as important as short-term goals. Change does not happen in a year. A district or school must be committed to a two- to three-year process and must keep the energy and momentum going without grabbing the next shiny new initiative.

SOME CRITICAL ADVICE

Much of the accomplishment of implementing student-led academic teams springs from the success of early adopters. The way those early implementing classrooms go, the whole school goes. If academic teaming stumbles with the early adopters, it is hard to get other teachers to then trust the initiative enough to attempt it. We urge school leaders to bring in expert advisors and research-based strategies to provide their school with the greatest advantage to succeed. Feel free to learn more about research-based resources from www.AcademicTeaming.com.

📄 **POINTS TO CONSIDER: CHAPTER 5**

This page is to jot down points from Chapter 5 to consider later and discuss with colleagues and students.

ACADEMIC TEAMING—MODEL INSTRUCTION FOR THE 21ST CENTURY

MASTER TEACHERS *OR* MASTER STUDENTS?

Research studies have consistently shown that the way to significantly improve a school, no matter how poor or great, is to improve the effectiveness of its teachers. Teacher effectiveness is at the very top of Hattie's meta-analysis of 195 factors that improve student achievement, with an exceptionally impressive effect size of *d* 5 1.57 (Hattie, 2015). Yet, the ability to rapidly improve instruction has proved to be an elusive goal. Substantial investments in teacher preparation reform, professional development systems, professional learning communities, instructional coaches, and even high-stakes teacher evaluation systems have not minted significantly more master teachers. Why? Perhaps it is because our entire definition of master teacher is incorrect.

When most of us envision a master teacher, we see a charismatic presenter with strong student relationships and a well-ordered classroom as the archetype. These are typically our Teacher of the Year winners. What if, instead, we defined a master teacher as one who creates a learning environment that develops *master students*? We would have to envision a completely different archetype, one where the teacher is often silent, acting as a master facilitator who allows the student-led academic teams to take center stage. Teams engage in lively debate, citing evidence-based claims and explaining their reasoning as they productively struggle with rigorous content applied to real-world scenarios. In this classroom environment, students develop prosocial skills, self-confidence, conflict resolution, empathy, and leadership, along with rigorous academic learning. They know how to self-manage and how to motivate and inspire others. This is a true 21st-century master teacher's classroom.

Most of us have heard of the 10,000-hour rule: It takes 10,000 hours, or nearly 10 years, of deliberate practice to develop mastery in a complex domain. This makes sense in the context of teacher-centered instruction, where the teacher does everything and is responsible for all learning in the classroom. The bigger the toolbox the teacher needs, the more time it will take to learn each tool with mastery. It is analogous to a master mechanic—one who has a giant multi-tiered toolbox filled with carefully ordered and polished tools. Master mechanics know how to use each one of these tools for specific situations that they diagnose in engines. In a similar way, traditional teachers need a large toolbox of research-based instructional strategies and must know how to use each one of these strategies to meet the diverse learning needs of students. A traditional, teacher-centered instructor needs hundreds, even thousands, of deliberate practice hours to become skilled with all the strategies necessary in today's diverse classrooms.

Contrast the scenario of the traditional teacher who struggles to master a huge toolbox of strategies and all the ways to use them with the pathway to mastery for a teacher who implements academic teaming. The academic teaming master teacher can have a much more focused toolbox because students begin to take responsibility for their own learning outcomes. The academic teaming master teacher provides strategies to his or her students and expects them to use the strategies with their peers as the teacher takes on the role of facilitator. The teacher essentially shifts to helping the students build their own toolbox of strategies and use them masterfully within their teams. Academic teaming structures are still complex and require work to get in place, but the pathway for establishing a learning environment that develops master students is *much* shorter than 10,000 hours. There is simply less for the teacher to master in an academic teaming classroom; the students are the ones developing mastery with the strategies. Learning becomes a *shared* effort, whereas in the traditional classroom, the teacher was responsible for nearly all the effort. The joint responsibility creates a more enjoyable teaching experience because the students put forth more effort, owning their own and their peers' learning outcomes in academic teams.

ACCELERATING TOWARD MASTERY WITH ACADEMIC TEAMING

On one of our visits to a middle school that was implementing academic teaming as part of the Schools for Rigor initiative, the principal wanted to show us an interesting example of a teacher's speedy progress to mastery. The principal brought us to the classrooms of two teachers with common planning who were teaching the same lesson. In the first classroom, the teacher was younger and had a posture and countenance that was somewhat serious and "military" in his bearing. During our short observation, he barely said a word. He walked among the academic teams, making notes and tracking students' progress toward the learning targets. The students never even looked up to see the visitors because they were so engaged in their teamwork, energetically reasoning with each other to solve the challenging task. At each table, every student was leaning in and engaged in the work.

Contrast this to the second classroom—a veteran teacher across the hall. When we walked in, all we heard was the teacher. He was more charismatic than the other teacher, and his students were attentive but passive. He would occasionally have students share their ideas with a partner, so there was some interaction and lower-level talk, but then he would bring it back to his lecture quickly to keep pace with his lesson. He was clearly attempting to drive the students' learning, unlike in the first classroom, where the students were doing that themselves.

Which one was further along as a master teacher with an environment to create master students? Interestingly, the principal said the younger teacher is only a third-year teacher and had struggled his entire first year with classroom management and student relationships. After implementing academic teaming for a year and half, what a difference we saw. He took to the methodology, setting up the group structures and releasing the tasks to students to form academic teams. This struggling teacher rapidly improved toward masterful when he moved from attempting to do everything himself to a structured release to the student teams, empowering the students in their learning.

MASTER TEACHERS DEVELOP MASTER TEAMS

Teachers simply cannot develop master students by lecturing to them. We need a new model. The new definition we propose is that master teachers create a learning environment with academic teaming that produces master students. The theory of action is that master teachers enable master academic teams that, in turn, develop master students. This means that a true master teacher must release to academic teams the rigorous tasks that create productive struggle so that students can indeed develop into master learners—gaining social, emotional, and cognitive skills in the process.

The critical point is that the level of mastery needed to reach SECL outcomes requires a different formula for creating both master teachers and master students (recall Figure 1.7). Teachers must have a student process (i.e., academic teaming) that allows the students to develop and practice these social and emotional skills while they are engaged in productive struggle to increase their cognitive skills. This relationship of teacher inputs and student process results in master learners.

THE POWER AND POTENTIAL OF ACADEMIC TEAMING AS A REFORM

The simple understanding that traditional pedagogy, where students passively receive instruction, does not create master students is incredibly powerful. It goes a long way to explaining why so many reforms have done so little to raise achievement and develop 21st-century learners. Many of these well-intended reforms were simply an overlay on traditional teaching; they

Academic Teaming Produces SECL Outcomes

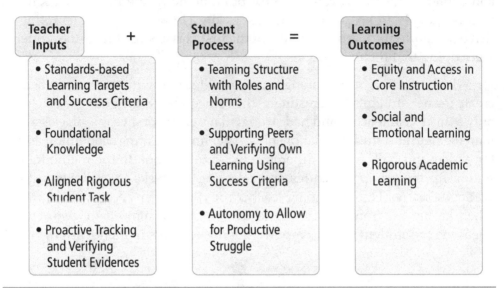

FIGURE 1.7. Academic teaming instructional model.

did not fundamentally change how teachers teach or how students learn. These reforms have contributed to a common phenomenon, initiative fatigue, where layer after layer of initiatives are added to teachers' responsibilities, with the expectation that somehow these initiatives will result in master students. In truth, focusing on a single initiative—implementing and cultivating student-led academic teaming—creates the social, emotional, and cognitive learning outcomes that many of the other initiatives aim for but fall short to manifest. Academic teaming is the missing process that has the power to transform how students learn and develop mastery of the skills they will need to thrive in the 21st century.

HOW DOES ACADEMIC TEAMING HELP TEACHERS?

Teachers report to us that one of the biggest benefits of academic teaming to them is the student ownership and the accountability it creates. Students have clear standards-based learning targets, success criteria, and rigorous tasks to accomplish within structures for self and peer accountability. Teachers explain how students are more engaged and better behaved. Many report that the very students who were the most challenging often became the best team leaders and that insecure learners now freely participate in their academic teams. A common teacher comment is that teaching is now more enjoyable because the students shoulder more responsibility and are more engaged with their teams.

HOW DOES ACADEMIC TEAMING HELP STUDENTS?

Students tell us they like coming to school more than they did before, feel they know their peers better, and are more accepted by their team members. Students from lower socio-economic environments often say they have newfound confidence in their abilities and pride in their learning as they experience more academic success. We often hear students talk about experiencing leadership in their teams and seeing new possibilities for themselves. Teachers and observers are taken aback by the level of care and empathy academic team members express with students of different abilities. Less confident students (i.e., those who do not raise their hands to answer questions) say they are more comfortable engaging and receiving support from their peers than from their teacher. Academic teaming creates more access for all learners, resulting in greater equity for students in core instruction.

HOW DOES ACADEMIC TEAMING HELP SCHOOLS?

Principals report that schoolwide behaviors improve as students learn self- and peer-regulation in academic teams and students are more cognitively engaged. Many principals tell us that teachers with higher-functioning academic teams typically have better test results than those who hold to a more traditional model of instruction. Principals report, and our research confirms, that students in subgroup categories in schools implementing academic teaming, compared to control groups not implementing academic teaming, are closing the achievement gaps. The biggest benefit according to principals is that their teachers and students are happier. The school culture improves significantly as the benefits of academic teaming manifest in classrooms and then spill over into the hallways and the rest of the school.

HOW DOES ACADEMIC TEAMING HELP PARENTS AND GUARDIANS?

Parents often tell principals and teachers, who in turn tell us, that their children are noticeably more mature and confident after learning within academic teaming environments. Children like going to school and are also more self-assured verbal communicators. This is quite an accomplishment in an era dominated by communication via impersonal texting.

Neuroscience helps explain what parents notice when their children are involved in academic teaming. Students whose brains get the endorphin-loaded euphoria of successfully solving a team problem are often eager to talk at home about their work at school. No more one-word answers to the parent's question, "How was school today?" This attitude improves their behavior at home. Meanwhile, parents are now less stressed about their child's achievement in school.

HOW DOES ACADEMIC TEAMING HELP TEACHER PREPARATION PROGRAMS?

Teacher preparation programs are under a great deal of pressure to develop effective new teachers for 21st-century classrooms. Asking the question "What skills do new teachers need to acquire in order to *develop* master students?" creates a different focus for teacher preparation.

Teacher preparation programs, for example, have historically focused on equipping new teachers to manage their first classrooms with teacher-centered classroom routines and strategies. Arguably, if new teachers cannot control their classrooms, they will not survive long as teachers. Classroom management skills are critical; however, when new teachers learn to successfully control their classrooms through teacher-centered methods, they likely will stay with these methods for much of their career.

If teacher preparation programs instead embraced equipping new teachers with student-centered classroom management routines and strategies, it would set new teachers on the student-centered pathway from the start. Equally important is redefining the roles of the teacher and the student in a student-centered classroom because many preservice teachers have never experienced this type of classroom as a student themselves. The student teacher internship could also be redesigned to prioritize placement of preservice teachers in the most student-centered classrooms available. The good news is that more of these classrooms will be available as more schools embrace academic teaming as their core instruction.

HOW DOES NEUROSCIENCE SUPPORT ACADEMIC TEAMING?

Throughout this book, we have referred to research from neuroscience that supports the benefits of academic teaming. Let us take another look at some of the important findings.

❖ **Whoever explains learns.** When students talk to their peers about what they are learning, it helps them make connections to what they already know, thereby strengthening and expanding neural networks. This process aids in generating meaning, thus increasing the likelihood that students will remember the new learning.

* **Recruiting additional brain areas.** The brain is genetically programmed to solve problems to help us survive. When faced with a new problem it has not previously encountered (as in productive struggle), the brain recruits previously uninvolved brain areas (as shown in brain scans), most likely to provide more neural input as well as opportunities to explore and evaluate new potential solutions. Students in the team get insights into the problem that they may not have had before.

* **The brain that does the work is the brain that learns.** In the teacher-centered classroom, the teacher is doing most of the cerebral work and processing the content once again. In the academic teaming classroom, students must engage and learn what they need to know to solve a given problem on their own. Their brains work harder, and they learn more.

* **Success stimulates the reward circuits.** When the students in academic teams feel a sense of belonging and peer support as they successfully achieve their learning targets, their brains release euphoria-producing substances, bringing them pleasure, emotional contentment, and a desire to repeat this activity in the future. This explains why students who did not find school enjoyable in the past now look forward to their academic teaming assignments.

* **Counteracting the negative effects of technology on developing thinking skills.** The increasing amount of time that students spend searching for answers on their digital devices is hindering their development of higher-order thinking skills. Because the use of these devices is either very limited or excluded in academic teams, students must use and develop their own brains to think through and solve problems rather than turn to the Internet for someone else's solution.

* **Counteracting the negative effects of technology on social skill development.** Because social media has greatly reduced face-to-face conversation between students, they are not learning the social skills necessary to constructively engage in discussion groups, respect differing opinions, or develop positive peer relationships. This is happening at a time when the adolescent brain is primed for prosocial growth. Academic teaming requires students to work productively in a group, thereby helping students develop listening skills, empathy, and a sense of equity rather than dominance.

* **Collaboration increases brain synchrony.** The more students collaborate during problem solving, the more their brain waves become synchronized. Students whose brain waves synchronized with each other were able to make decisions and solve problems more efficiently

HOW DOES ACADEMIC TEAMING HELP POLICY MAKERS?

Many state- and district-level policy makers have embraced the idea of SEL skill development for all students and closing the achievement gaps. Yet, the *how* to do this remains elusive and often at the school level means bringing in yet another program that does not substantively change the role of teaching and learning in core instruction. Are our school improvement plans, for example, designed to support our teachers to *develop* master students? Just asking this one question in every policy application could have a tremendous impact on school reform.

FINAL THOUGHTS

This book shows the promise and research for academic teaming to transform schools and classrooms into social, emotional, and cognitive learning environments that develop master students. This promise is rooted in academic teaming implementations that result in high-functioning student-led teams. The classroom culture will transform into an SECL environment as classrooms move from predominately lecture and independent practice to academic teaming. In these transformed classrooms, there is a blend of direct instruction and academic teaming, with most of the typical lessons structured to allow students to engage in challenging thinking tasks in their academic teams. Greater benefits emerge as the students learn to operate with increased autonomy from the teacher within their academic teams and rely on their teams for support. The teacher can then switch roles, becoming a facilitator, thus gaining the much-needed time to track students' progress on achieving standards-based learning targets and to provide personalized micro-interventions as necessary to ensure all students reach the learning targets.

At the Learning Sciences Applied Research Center, we have proficiently taken more than 1,000 classrooms across the nation through this transformation. We have created and validated research-based techniques to help support teachers through this journey to high-functioning academic teams. We have also cataloged the common errors and issues that can impede schoolwide implementations or individual classrooms. Our companion website, www.AcademicTeaming.com, gives educators access to resources, videos, tools, professional development, leadership coaching, and monitoring metrics to help on the journey to successfully implementing and receiving the many benefits of academic teaming for teachers and students.

We wish teachers and students well on their journey to student-led academic teaming core instruction.

📄 POINTS TO CONSIDER: CONCLUSION

This page is to jot down points from the Conclusion to consider later and discuss with colleagues and students.

APPENDICES

The Appendices provide information to deepen understanding of the relationship between academic teaming and other educational frameworks, initiatives, and skills deemed crucial for success in today's world. The crosswalk documents explain the alignment between academic teaming and other programs and principles, such as social and emotional learning, equity and access, growth mindset, and classroom formative assessment. Other resources provided demonstrate how academic teaming supports the development of a broad set of skills, work habits, character traits, and mindsets in students.

APPENDIX A

CROSSWALK FOR CASEL'S SEL COMPETENCIES AND ACADEMIC TEAMING

The Collaborative for Academic, Social, and Emotional Learning (CASEL) describes social and emotional learning (SEL) as the means through which students learn to regulate their own emotions, self- and peer-motivate to reach their goals, exercise empathy, work together effectively, and engage in responsible decision making. CASEL's framework identifies five core competencies and 25 subcompetencies for SEL, shown below. In the right column, we specify how academic teaming supports each of CASEL's SEL competencies and subcompetencies.

How CASEL's 25 Social and Emotional Learning Competencies Align to Student-Led Academic Teaming

Core SEL Competency: Self-Awareness The ability to accurately recognize one's own emotions, thoughts, and values and how they influence behavior. The ability to accurately assess one's strengths and limitations with a well-grounded sense of confidence, optimism, and a "growth mindset."	
Subcompetencies (Descriptors) for Self-Awareness	**Alignment to Academic Teaming**
1. Identifying emotions	Team interactions and discussions create a classroom environment where students can articulate how they think and feel. Team protocols include identification of emotions along with protocols for self-management of emotions and peer regulation of emotions. *See Chapter 2 for an example of a teacher coaching a student team to identify their own and others' emotions.*
2. Accurate self-perception	Students develop a sound awareness of their own abilities through constant self-assessment and peer feedback in their academic teams.
3. Recognizing strengths	Academic teaming allows students to assess their own and others' strengths and find ways to use their collective abilities to tackle rigorous tasks.
4. Self-confidence	Students build confidence and a growth mindset within their teams by discovering they can contribute value to the team and by being accepted by their peers.
5. Self-efficacy	Teaming structures, such as roles and norms, allow students to build autonomy so they can work through rigorous academic content with limited teacher assistance. *See Chapter 4 for a student's reflection on how teaming empowers her to rely less on her teacher and makes her feel more optimistic about her learning.*

Core SEL Competency: Self-Management
The ability to successfully regulate one's emotions, thoughts, and behaviors in different situations—effectively managing stress, controlling impulses, and motivating oneself. The ability to set and work toward personal and academic goals.

Subcompetencies (Descriptors) for Self-Management	Alignment to Academic Teaming
6. Impulse control	Team norms help students autonomously manage their behavior and stay focused on their team's tasks.
7. Stress management	Academic teaming structures create a network of peer support where students can manage their own stress and help each other through frustrations. *See Chapter 4 for various student reflections on how teaming helps them manage stress.*
8. Self-discipline	Academic teaming fosters a naturally disciplined classroom environment where students rise to the high academic expectations of their teacher and learn to self-regulate their behavior.
9. Self-motivation	Teaming structures allow students to take responsibility for their own learning as they tackle highly engaging academic problems with their peers.
10. Goal setting	In their teams, students use standards-based guidelines created by the teacher (learning targets and success criteria) to set academic goals. Teams track their own progress and use peer feedback to make adjustments as they work to achieve their goals.
11. Organizational skills	Students plan and organize their resources, time, and each other to accomplish rigorous learning tasks.

Core SEL Competency: Social Awareness
The ability to take the perspective of and empathize with others, including those from diverse backgrounds and cultures. The ability to understand social and ethical norms for behavior and to recognize family, school, and community resources and supports.

Subcompetencies (Descriptors) for Social Awareness	Alignment to Academic Teaming
12. Perspective-taking	In forming academic teams, teachers aim to create a diverse mix of cultures, races, genders, abilities, personalities, and learning needs. Students learn to listen and respond to each other's unique perspectives through team tasks. *See Chapter 4 for an associate superintendent's take on how teaming allows his district's students to bring their diverse personal experiences into their learning.*

13. Empathy	Students learn how their teammates think and feel through team interactions and provide peer support, allowing students to better understand and connect with their peers to reach authentic empathy.
14. Appreciating diversity	Academic teaming creates an inclusive learning environment where students can appreciate the different backgrounds and strengths of their peers.
15. Respect for others	Working in academic teams allows students to connect with each other on a deeper level and create relationships of respect. *See Chapter 4 for a teacher's story of how her student, who previously struggled with negative behavior, led his teammates respectfully and became respected by his peers.*

Core SEL Competency: Relationship Skills
The ability to establish and maintain healthy and rewarding relationships with diverse individuals and groups. The ability to communicate clearly, listen well, cooperate with others, resist inappropriate social pressure, negotiate conflict constructively, and seek and offer help when needed.

Subcompetencies (Descriptors) for Relationship Skills	Alignment to Academic Teaming
16. Communication	Academic teams have clear norms for communication, which ensure respectful discussions with equal contributions from each team member. *See Chapter 2 for a classroom example of how students used communication guidelines in their teams to have a constructive conversation with autonomy.*
17. Social engagement	With their academic teams, students have constant opportunities to develop cooperation skills and conflict resolution skills. Engaging with their peers also helps students build the confidence to be assertive in resisting negative social pressure.
18. Relationship building	Academic teaming helps students build healthy peer support networks, where they can feel safe to seek and offer help.
19. Teamwork	Academic team tasks are designed for productive struggle, where students rely on each other to accomplish their learning goals and coach each other through challenges with limited teacher direction.

Core SEL Competency: Responsible Decision Making
The ability to make constructive choices about personal behavior and social interactions based on ethical standards, safety concerns, and social norms. The realistic evaluation of consequences of various actions and a consideration of the well-being of oneself and others.

Subcompetencies (Descriptors) for Responsible Decision Making	Alignment to Academic Teaming
20. Identifying problems	Academic teaming empowers students to use their norms to identify problems in social situations and to use success criteria and peer feedback to identify problems in their academic tasks.
21. Analyzing situations	Academic teaming structures foster autonomy, so teams constantly practice analyzing their academic tasks and their social situations and can learn to make responsible decisions.
22. Solving problems	Within their teams, students engage in both academic problem solving and interpersonal conflict resolution.
23. Evaluating	In academic teams, students are expected to fulfill their roles and constantly evaluate whether they are making responsible decisions. *See Chapter 2 for an example of a student evaluating his teammates' behavior and deciding he needed to get them refocused on the task.*
24. Reflecting	Teaming structures encourage students to give and receive feedback, consistently reflecting on their thoughts, actions, decisions, and progress to goals.
25. Ethical responsibility	Teaming structures build a culture and mindset of accountability, where students learn to take responsibility for themselves and their actions and interact with fairness. *See Chapter 1 for a teacher's experience of how academic teaming brings out a level of care and concern she has never before seen in her middle school students.*

Adapted from CASEL (2017). Please note: the five competencies and 25 subcompetencies (left column) are CASEL's work; the alignment of the competencies to student-led academic teaming (right column) was done by the authors of this book, independently of CASEL.

APPENDIX B

CROSSWALK FOR HARVARD'S SEL SKILLS AND ACADEMIC TEAMING

The Wallace Foundation funded a team of researchers at the Harvard Graduate School of Education to produce a report that would examine various SEL programs across the United States. The researchers categorized the major SEL skills and behaviors and developed a list of 12 social and emotional skills linked to positive academic, interpersonal, and mental health outcomes. The information provided in the left and middle columns in the table below is adapted from *Navigating SEL from the Inside Out* by Jones et al. (2017, pp. 314–323). In the right column, we specify how academic teaming supports and aligns with each of these skills.

12 Social and Emotional Skills Linked to Child Outcomes
from a Harvard Study funded by the Wallace Foundation

Alignment to Student-Led Academic Teaming

Cognitive Skills		
1. Attention Control	The ability to attend to relevant information and goal-directed tasks while resisting distractions and shifting tasks when necessary, such as listening to the teacher and ignoring kids outside on the playground.	In an active academic teaming environment, classroom noise is natural, as multiple conversations happen at once and students leave their seats to retrieve resources or check information posted around the room. In teams, students are able to practice attention control consistently; teaming structures promote self-monitoring and include norms for helping refocus peers' attention if the team starts to get off task.
2. Working Memory and Planning Skills	Working memory refers to the ability to cognitively maintain and manipulate information over a relatively short period of time, and planning skills are used to identify and organize the steps or sequence of events needed to complete an activity and achieve a desired goal.	In academic teams, students build the cognitive capacity to tackle complex, multi-step tasks. Students are expected to use standards-based guidelines designed by their teacher (learning targets and success criteria) to plan, organize, and track their own learning with their teams and achieve their academic goals.

3. Inhibitory Control	The ability to suppress or modify a behavioral response in service of attaining a longer-term goal by inhibiting automatic reactions, such as shouting out an answer, while initiating controlled responses appropriate to the situation, such as remembering to raise one's hand.	Teaming structures, such as communication tools and norms, remind students to refrain from automatic reactions, such as interrupting peers or dominating conversations. As teams become high functioning, students internalize these norms and exercise inhibitory control as a second-nature response.
4. Cognitive Flexibility	The ability to switch between thinking about two different concepts to thinking about multiple concepts simultaneously, or to redirect one's attention away from one salient object, instruction, or strategy to another.	As students engage in authentic problem solving with their teams, they must switch attention between various information sources, ideas, and strategies as they listen to their teammates and analyze different opinions. Rigorous team tasks require students to generate and test their own hypotheses in collaboration with their peers, helping them build fluid cognitive abilities.
Emotional Skills		
5. Emotion Knowledge and Expression	The ability to recognize, understand, and label emotions in oneself and others (emotion knowledge) and to express one's feelings in contextually appropriate ways (emotion expression).	Academic teaming structures encourage students to verbalize and analyze their own and others' thoughts and feelings. Working in teams gives students the opportunity to communicate personal experiences to their peers and connect those experiences to the academic content. Teaming builds a classroom culture where students support and care for one another and can feel safe to express emotion.

6. Emotion and Behavior Regulation	The ability to use effortful control strategies to modify the intensity or duration of emotional arousal, both positive and negative (emotion regulation), as well as the ability to learn and conform to expectations for appropriate social behavior (behavior regulation).	Team norms and consistent social interactions within teams help students learn and exercise appropriate behaviors. Productive struggle through rigorous team tasks places students in challenging situations where they build skills to cope with and overcome negative feelings without acting inappropriately. Through consistent opportunities to verbalize thoughts, feelings, and opinions within their teams, students can become more mindful of their emotions and learn to regulate them.
7. Empathy and Perspective-Taking	The ability to understand another person's emotional state and point of view. This includes identifying, acknowledging, and acting upon the experiences, feelings, and viewpoints of others, whether by placing oneself in another's situation or through the vicarious experiencing of another's emotions.	Working closely with peers in academic teams exposes students to unique perspectives and gives students the opportunity to exercise active listening. Students learn to appreciate the diverse viewpoints of their teammates; teaming helps students build empathy by deepening their emotional understanding of and connection to their peers.
Interpersonal Skills		
8. Understanding Social Cues	The process through which children interpret cues from their social environment and use them to understand the behaviors of others.	In interacting with peers on a daily basis within their academic teams, students are able to practice interpreting, responding to, and using social cues. Talking through thought processes via team tasks allows teammates to understand the motivations and intentions behind their own and their teammates' thoughts and actions.

9. Conflict Resolution/ Social Problem Solving	The ability to generate and act on effective strategies or solutions for challenging interpersonal situations and conflicts.	In academic teams, students are expected to follow norms and practice effective strategies for communicating respectfully, which can prevent interpersonal conflict from occurring in the first place. When conflicts do occur, teaming structures and protocols help students resolve interpersonal conflicts as a team, often without teacher interventions; these structures also guide students in determining when they do need to involve an adult.
10. Prosocial Skills	The skills required to organize and navigate social relationships, including the ability to interact effectively with others and develop positive relationships. This includes a broad range of skills and behaviors, such as listening/ communication, cooperation, helping, community building, and being a good friend.	Academic teaming helps students build positive relationships with their peers and become part of a community of learners. The authenticity of working together to tackle rigorous academic challenges helps students to bond with their peers and recognize them as valuable contributing members of their learning community. Students actively participate in communicating, cooperating, and supporting one another through teaming and are also able to exercise leadership and followership.
Additional Skills		
11. Character	A set of culturally determined skills, values, and habits required to understand, care about, and act upon core ethical values (e.g., respect, justice, citizenship, responsibility for self and others) and to perform to one's highest potential in achievement or work contexts, such as perseverance, diligence, and self-control.	In academic teams, students are expected to perform their roles, fulfill their commitments to the team to their best ability, and treat others with respect and empathy. Students have the autonomy to make their own decisions and hold themselves and their teammates accountable to high academic and behavioral standards. Teaming helps students develop a real-world understanding of why they need to exercise strong character because they can see the impact each person has on the team.

12. Mindset	Attitudes and beliefs about oneself, others, and one's own circumstances that impact one's interpretation of and response to events and interactions throughout one's day.	Academic teaming helps students feel empowered in their learning. Students track and celebrate their progress with their teammates, developing a growth mindset because they can see that dedication and hard work will help them succeed. Productive struggle within team tasks builds resiliency to protect against negative feelings and fosters self-confidence and a positive attitude.

Adapted from Jones et al. (2017, pp. 314–323). Please note: the 12 skills (left column) and their descriptions (middle column) are the work of Jones et al.; the alignment of these skills to student-led academic teaming (right column) was done by the authors of this book, independently of Jones et al.

APPENDIX C

KEY 21ST-CENTURY SKILLS

The term *21st-century skills* is widely used in education and generally references the skills, work habits, and character traits commonly desired in today's and tomorrow's workplaces. The table below highlights some of these skills that have been identified by various organizations. We bolded some of the most frequently mentioned skills across all organizations—note their close alignment to academic teaming.

Selected List of 21st-Century Skills from Different Organizations

Organization	Skills
Common Core State Standards (for literacy, mathematics)	Cogent reasoning Evidence collection **Critical thinking, problem solving, analytical skills** **Communication**
Partnership for 21st-Century Learning	**Critical thinking and problem solving** Creativity and innovation **Cross-cultural understanding** **Communications**, information, and media literacy Computing and Information and Communication Technology (ICT) literacy Career and learning self-reliance **Collaboration**
Harvard Graduate School of Education: Seven Survival Skills	**Critical thinking and problem solving** **Collaboration** Agility and adaptability Initiative and entrepreneurialism **Effective oral and written communication** Accessing and analyzing information Curiosity and imagination
Organization for Economic Cooperation and Development (OECD)	Using tools interactively **Interacting in heterogeneous groups** Acting autonomously

American Association of Colleges and Universities (AACU)	Writing **Critical thinking** Quantitative reasoning **Oral communication** **Intercultural skills** Information literacy Ethical reasoning **Analytic reasoning** Research skills and projects Integration of learning across disciplines Application of learning beyond the classroom Civic engagement and competence
International Society for Technology in Education (ISTE)	Creativity and innovation **Communication and collaboration** Research and information fluency **Critical thinking, problem solving, and decision making** Digital citizenship Technology operations and concepts
World Economic Forum	**Critical thinking/problem solving** **Communication** **Collaboration** Creativity Initiative Persistence/grit Adaptability Curiosity Leadership **Social and cultural awareness**

Sources: AACU (2017); Council of Chief State School Officers (2018); Harvard Graduate School of Education (2016); ISTE (2018); National Education Association (2018); OECD (2018); World Economic Forum (2015).

APPENDIX D

CROSSWALK FOR GROWTH MINDSET AND ACADEMIC TEAMING

Psychologist Carol Dweck introduced the power of mindset and its impact on learning and achievement in *Mindset: The New Psychology of Success* in 2006. Her belief is that students with a fixed mindset may achieve less than their potential while students with a growth mindset can reach ever-higher levels of achievement. The table below provides information on mindset and how it relates to academic teaming. The left and middle columns identify the differences between a fixed mindset and a growth mindset, taken directly from Dweck's (2006) work. In the right column in the table, we specify how academic teaming provides opportunities to generate and cultivate a growth mindset in students.

Fixed Mindset *Intelligence is static* Leads to a desire to look smart and therefore a tendency to . . .	Growth Mindset *Intelligence can be developed* Leads to a desire to learn and therefore a tendency to . . .	Student-Led Academic Teaming Develops a Growth Mindset
. . . avoid challenges	. . . embrace challenges	In their academic teams, students are expected to embrace challenges together, rather than depend on the teacher to rescue them.
. . . get defensive or give up easily	. . . persist in the face of obstacles	Productive struggle, a key component of academic teaming, builds students' resilience as they rely on each other to overcome social, emotional, and cognitive obstacles.
. . . see effort as fruitless or worse	. . . see effort as the path to mastery	Students track their own and their academic team's progress and can see their effort paying off as they reach their learning goals. Academic teaming gives students multiple opportunities to practice skills and demonstrate mastery in real-world tasks.

. . . ignore useful negative feedback	. . . learn from criticism	Academic teaming creates a classroom environment of constant feedback, where students push each other's thinking and learn to give constructive criticism.
. . . feel threatened by the success of others	. . . find lessons and inspiration in the success of others	Academic teaming creates a culture of collaboration, rather than competition. Students learn to support each other and celebrate their team's success.

Adapted from Dweck (2006, p. 263). Please note: the fixed mindset descriptions (left column) and growth mindset descriptions (middle column) are the work of Dweck; the alignment of these descriptions to student-led academic teaming (right column) was done by the authors of this book, independently of Dweck.

APPENDIX E

CROSSWALK FOR EQUITY PRINCIPLES AND ACADEMIC TEAMING

In *Designing for Equity: Leveraging Competency-Based Education to Ensure All Students Succeed* (2018), Sturgis and Casey introduce nine equity principals in a framework to guide districts and schools to create an equitable system that effectively serves all students. Descriptions of these nine principles are included on the left side of the table below. We specify how academic teaming supports and aligns with each of these principles in the right column of the table.

Equity Principles	Equity in Student-Led Academic Teaming
1. Nurture Strong Culture of Learning and Inclusivity District and school cultures ensure all students and adults, especially the most marginalized, feel safe and respected. They are intentionally designed to build trusting relationships that promote positive identity and enable direct and productive feedback. Adults regularly share their own learning and model a growth mindset for students. Students unfamiliar with a school's dominant culture may lack fluency in the social cues and language that educators use to interpret students' readiness for learning. Acknowledging the existence of a dominant culture is important in order to open dialogue regarding student communication and engagement. Students are supported in becoming independent learners. Educators have the autonomy to be responsive to students as they progress, and distributed leadership strategies empower staff to make decisions based on what is best for students.	**Students build strong social bonds with their peers and experience belonging in their academic teams.** Academic teaming structures are designed for social bonding—students work in diverse teams with norms that ensure every student has the chance to contribute equitably to their team, can feel safe through peer support, and can develop a growth mindset. The teacher can focus on monitoring teams and develops a heightened sense of student needs. In high-functioning academic teams, students meet each other's needs with limited teacher guidance and experience self-actualization through caring for their peers as much as they care about themselves.

2. Engage the Community in Shaping New Definitions of Success and Graduation Outcomes

Districts and schools engage their community in creating a shared vision of what students need to know and be able to do for future success. They take proactive steps to be sure that all voices—particularly those that have been historically marginalized—are included and elevated. Through these dialogues and leveraging research about the learning sciences, districts and schools define well-rounded competencies that all students will master upon graduation. Their definition of student success includes but is not limited to what it means to be college and career ready: they integrate academic knowledge, the skills to transfer and apply that knowledge, and a set of lifelong learning skills that enable students to be independent learners. Because students have different strengths, interests, and aspirations, districts and schools may allow for multiple pathways to success and multiple methods of demonstrating success. However, they balance this flexibility with rigorous commitment to ensuring all pathways and all demonstrations are equally reflective of the competencies that define success. Beyond simply defining success, districts and schools create a culture of learning in which all stakeholders internalize and value their shared vision of success and commit to shared accountability for ensuring that all students achieve it.

Academic teaming outcomes create a vision for the community of all students building the skills they will need to be successful after graduation.

In their academic teams, students work toward becoming college and career ready through developing and deepening academic skills, social-emotional skills, and 21st-century skills. Rigorous team tasks give students the opportunity to apply and transfer their skills and knowledge to various real-world contexts across all subjects. Since students become naturally engaged in the challenging academic work and have autonomy with their teams, their self-motivation increases, and students can develop into lifelong learners. Schools can showcase these positive student outcomes in order to collaborate with the community to promote a vision around the power of academic teaming. Students are empowered to assert their voices in the classroom, which can translate to asserting themselves to make a positive difference in their schools and communities.

3. Invest in Adult Mindsets, Knowledge, and Skills	Schools that implement academic teaming engage educators in instructional coaching, instructional rounds, and professional learning communities.
Leadership values and supports the ongoing growth of adults. Trust is actively nurtured. Structures provide ongoing opportunities for nurturing growth mindset and self-reflection. Adults deepen awareness of their own cultural identities, seek to understand their students, and proactively address bias. Teachers are supported in building their professional skills in the learning sciences, instructional strategies, knowledge of the domains, learning progressions, and equity strategies, including cultural responsiveness and Universal Design for Learning.	The benefits of student-led academic teaming give schools a vision to rally around as they engage in the transformation from traditional instruction to academic teaming. This process of change is self-reflective by nature and can help build growth mindset in educators. School leaders who have successfully shifted their schools to academic teaming align their support systems so educators can give each other feedback and collaborate on teaching practices and analyzing student evidence. Teachers are better able to understand students on a deep level and to evaluate their own preconceptions of students when teachers are gathering minute-to-minute student evidence and discussing this data with other teachers. Teachers can more easily see themselves as agents of transformation as they analyze evidence of their impact on students' learning and lives.
4. Establish Transparency About Learning, Progress, and Pace	Student-led academic teaming involves transparent learning targets made accessible to students and a constant stream of student evidence for teachers to use in verifying student progress.
Learning cycles are explicit and transparent so that students, families, and other key stakeholders know what students need to learn, what proficiency looks like, how they will be assessed, and how they are progressing. Teachers work together to use data on student progress to respond to students and to inform their professional learning.	In classrooms that implement student-led academic teaming, the teacher provides standards-based guidelines (learning targets and success criteria), which are posted in the classroom for all students to see. Students use the success criteria to track their own progress and their teammates' progress toward learning targets with autonomy. Academic teaming creates a constant feedback loop amongst students and between students and the teacher; teachers gather student evidence on a daily basis. Teachers then use this student data to inform lesson planning and make on-the-spot instructional adjustments. The shared pedagogical philosophy, shared language, and shared vision that academic teaming provides helps teachers stay in sync when collaborating in their professional learning communities.

5. Monitor and Respond to Student Progress, Proficiency, and Pace	**Academic teaming helps all students reach proficiency through access to peer coaching, teacher support, and tools for self-tracking.**
Individual student pace and progress are closely monitored, as are trends over time by individuals and cohorts. Student progress is measured by growth along a learning continuum. Strategies are personalized to ensure each student sets and sustains a pace of learning that leads him or her toward graduation, with supports in place that ensure all students reach proficiency.	Academic teaming structures ensure self-tracking, peer tracking, and teacher tracking with transparent success criteria to measure each student's learning progress. Students learn to support each other in their academic teams, and the teacher has more time to spend with individual students who need extra support. Teachers can make on-the-spot adjustments to ensure all students are on the path to proficiency and graduation. Students can access more support through academic teaming than they could have accessed in a traditional classroom.
6. Respond and Adapt to Students Using Continuous Improvement Processes	**Teachers who implement academic teaming use leading student data to make on-the-spot adjustments.**
Districts and schools use data on student progress to create agile organizations that can respond to student needs, drive continuous improvement, and ensure that students are successfully reaching proficiency each step of the way. Data can also be used to seek out inequitable practices, identify and examine bias, and challenge predictability of success based on demographic factors.	Academic teaming makes student evidence visible—when students are discussing and debating the academic content, teachers are able to observe students' thinking. Teachers can adapt instruction in a timely manner to keep all students on track, which narrows the daily learning gap and in turn narrows the achievement gap. Teachers can also make well-informed decisions about how to group students based on daily student data. Teachers who begin to use academic teaming are often surprised by how well their historically low-performing students learn in their teams, leading to confrontation of biases.

7. Develop Shared Pedagogical Philosophy Based on Learning Sciences Districts and schools are designed around shared and explicit pedagogical philosophies based on research in the learning sciences, including neuroscience, engagement, motivation, and child/youth development. Important pedagogical approaches to include are school designs that support consistent relationships, Universal Design for Learning, culturally responsive strategies, and nurturing the skills for student agency.	**Schools that implement academic teaming use research-based strategies around a shared pedagogy.** Academic teaming has the power to transform schools and districts by uniting educators under a clear and proven pedagogical model. Academic teaming is based on research in educational neuroscience and is backed by field results with proven increases in achievement, social-emotional skills, positive behavior, engagement, and student ownership.
8. Support Students in Building Skills for Agency Agency allows individuals to take purposeful and meaningful action in pursuit of their goals and aspirations. It is a vitally important aspect of lifelong learning, and it is actively cultivated in competency-based systems. Schools are designed to develop the mindsets, motivation, and skills that comprise agency. Mindsets include a belief in one's own efficacy and locus of control to affect change. Motivation includes a genuine purpose for learning, intrinsic motivation, and persistent effort. Skills include self-regulation, metacognition, social and emotional skills, and specific academic behaviors. Culture and learning environments offer students multiple opportunities to practice and receive feedback in developing mindsets and skills.	**Academic teaming allows students to lead their own teams, drive their own learning, and develop autonomy.** Student agency and ownership are bedrocks of academic teaming. Teachers give student teams autonomy as they work on highly engaging, challenging team tasks. These tasks are designed to be purposeful, offer multiple opportunities to master skills and knowledge, and promote productive struggle, building resilience and confidence. Students have the opportunity to set learning goals and develop their intrinsic motivation as they step up to take accountability for themselves and for their teammates. Teaming structures such as norms explicitly teach students the skills for conflict resolution and self-efficacy.

9. Ensure Consistency of Expectations and Understanding of Proficiency	Academic teaming allows all students to experience rigorous instruction with clear expectations.
Expectations of learning targets and rigor are moderated with all students being held to the same high standards, including demonstrating mastery and fluency in the foundational skills.	Students who may not have previously been active participants in their own learning are able to access learning targets with their academic teams through high teacher expectations, consistent support, and multiple chances to demonstrate proficiency. All students can experience rigorous learning and frequent feedback through academic teaming.

Adapted from Sturgis & Casey (2018). Please note: the nine principles and their descriptions (left column) are the work of Sturgis & Casey; the alignment of these principles to student-led academic teaming (right column) was done by the authors of this book, independently of Sturgis & Casey.

APPENDIX F

CROSSWALK FOR THE FIVE STRATEGIES OF FORMATIVE ASSESSMENT TO ACADEMIC TEAMING

The five strategies of formative assessment, developed by Siobhan Leahy, Christine Lyon, Marnie Thompson, and Dylan Wiliam (2005) and outlined in *Embedding Formative Assessment: Practical Techniques for K–12 Classrooms* (Wiliam & Leahy, 2015), guide teachers and students to make minute-by-minute adjustments in instruction and learning to improve student outcomes. Formative assessment flourishes in the student-led academic teaming instructional model. In the following chart, the left column contains the five strategies; we detail how academic teaming aligns with each formative assessment strategy in the right column.

Formative Assessment Strategies	Alignment to Academic Teaming
1. Clarifying, sharing, and understanding learning intentions and success criteria	In the academic teaming model, all tasks are structured with learning targets (intentions) and success criteria. Teachers and students take joint responsibility for the learning. The teacher clarifies and shares the learning targets and success criteria with his or her students to give them a clear understanding of what mastery looks like and how they will get there; students then use the learning targets and success criteria to demonstrate their understanding of the content and to verify their learning.
2. Engineering effective discussion, tasks, and activities that elicit evidence of learning	Academic teaming makes student learning visible; the teacher can see evidence from all students (rather than from just those students who raise their hands in a traditional classroom). The teacher narrows daily learning gaps by tracking students' work in teams and can make instructional adjustments based on what students know and do not know or can and cannot do. The teacher develops a better understanding of each student's needs and can use this information when engineering rigorous tasks.

3. Providing feed-back that moves learning forward	Academic teaming builds a classroom culture of trust, growth mindset, and high motivation; students thus become more receptive to feedback for improvement. The teacher provides feedback to students to advance learning, and the academic teaming structure also encourages students to give feedback to each other. Team norms and supports provided by the teacher ensure that students have guidelines for giving each other clear, constructive peer feedback and celebrating one another's success.
4. Activating students as learning resources for one another	Academic teaming creates a structure where students peer teach, peer coach, and peer assess, becoming invaluable resources to one another. In academic teams, students are responsible for not only their own learning, but also for the learning of their peers. Each student has a role in the team and is held individually accountable for the team's success. Students help one another grow, benefiting both those who are giving help and those who are receiving help.
5. Activating students as owners of their own learning	In the academic teaming model, students are empowered to take ownership of their own learning. Academic teams are designed to make students gradually more self-reliant, needing less and less help from the teacher. Engaging, rigorous tasks develop an appetite for learning in all students and prepare students to enter the workforce as lifelong learners. In academic teaming, students are able to see how their learning connects to the real world and how effort leads to success.

Adapted from Wiliam & Leahy (2015). Please note: the five formative assessment strategies (left column) are the work of Leahy et al. (2005); the alignment of these strategies to student-led academic teaming (right column) was done by the authors of this book and reviewed by Wiliam.

APPENDIX G

CROSSWALK FOR THE SEVEN STRATEGIES OF ASSESSMENT FOR LEARNING TO ACADEMIC TEAMING

The following seven strategies were developed by Richard J. Stiggins, Judith A. Arter, Jan Chappuis, and Stephen Chappuis and are included in *Classroom Assessment for Student Learning: Doing it Right—Using it Well* (2004) and *Seven Strategies of Assessment* for *Learning* (Chappuis, 2010). These strategies of assessment FOR learning help students answer the three questions:

1. Where Am I Going?
2. Where Am I Now?
3. How Can I Close the Gap?

Assessment FOR learning is a natural component of the student-led academic teaming model because both teachers and students engage in this formative assessment process on a daily basis. In the following chart, the left and middle columns contain the seven strategies of assessment FOR learning and their descriptions; we created the right column in collaboration with Richard J. Stiggins to detail the alignment of academic teaming to each strategy.

Seven Strategies of Assessment FOR Learning	Descriptions	Alignment to Academic Teaming
Strategy 1: Provide students with a clear and understandable vision of the learning target.	Motivation and achievement both increase when instruction is guided by clearly defined targets. Activities that help students answer the question, "What's the learning target?" set the stage for all further formative assessment actions.	Learning targets are a fundamental component of the student-led academic teaming model. Teachers create clear learning targets based on the academic standards. In their teams, students use learning targets as goals to drive their learning in every lesson.

Strategy 2: Use examples and models of strong and weak work.	Carefully chosen examples of the range of quality can create and refine students' understanding of the learning goal by helping students answer the questions, "What defines quality work?" and "What are some problems to avoid?"	In academic teaming, students use success criteria as a tool to help them understand and plan for strong work. Success criteria provide students with a clear picture of the quality of work they should be able to demonstrate once they master the learning target and allow them to track their progress toward the learning target.
Strategy 3: Offer regular descriptive feedback.	Effective feedback shows students where they are on their path to attaining the intended learning. It answers for students the questions, "What are my strengths?" "What do I need to work on?" and "Where did I go wrong, and what can I do about it?"	In their academic teams, students verify their own and their team members' progress toward and achievement of the learning targets. The teacher continuously verifies student evidence and provides feedback and support to students as necessary. This verification process happens as students work, so students and teachers have time to make adaptations based on feedback before the lesson ends.
Strategy 4: Teach students to self-assess and set goals.	The information provided in effective feedback models the kind of evaluative thinking we want students to be able to do themselves. Strategy 4 teaches students to identify their strengths and weaknesses and to set goals for further learning. It helps them answer the questions, "What am I good at?" "What do I need to work on?" and "What should I do next?"	Academic teaming empowers students to self-track their progress to goals. Teachers give students the autonomy to drive their own learning through students using learning targets and success criteria to accomplish team tasks. Students become more self-aware in their teams as they learn to identify their own strengths, weaknesses, and personal goals for learning and to support their team members in doing the same.

Strategy 5: Design lessons to focus on one learning target or aspect of quality at a time.	When assessment information identifies a need, we can adjust instruction to target that need. In this strategy, we scaffold learning by narrowing the focus of a lesson to help students master a specific learning goal or to address specific misconceptions or problems.	The academic teaming model is designed to be responsive to student needs. Teachers can adjust their lessons based on student evidence and focus on specific learning targets or aspects of learning targets in order to address misconceptions and help students fill in gaps.
Strategy 6: Teach students focused revision.	This is a companion to Strategy 5—when a concept, skill, or competence proves difficult for students, we can let them practice it in smaller segments and give them feedback on just the aspects they are practicing. This strategy allows students to revise their initial work with a focus on a manageable number of learning targets or aspects of quality.	In the academic teaming model, students engage in productive struggle, with teams, constantly revising their thinking and deepening their learning. Students have multiple opportunities to demonstrate proficiency, practice, and revise based on feedback. The teaming structure makes it easier for this process to be focused on what each individual student or team needs and allows the teacher to more easily identify struggling students and ensure they get the help that they need.
Strategy 7: Engage students in self-reflection and let them keep track of and share their learning.	Long-term retention and motivation increase when students track, reflect on, and communicate about their learning. In this strategy, students look back on their journey, reflecting on their learning and sharing their achievement with others.	Academic teams are designed for students to track, reflect on, and communicate their learning. Learning targets and success criteria help students see their progress. The collaborative environment of academic teaming classrooms allows students to share their achievement with each other and celebrate one another's success.

Adapted from Chappuis, (2010, pp. 11–13). Please note: the seven strategies and their descriptions (left and middle columns) are the work of Stiggins et al. (2004); the alignment of these strategies to student-led academic teaming (right column) was done by the authors of this book in collaboration with Richard J. Stiggins.

APPENDIX H

CROSSWALK FOR OLD AND NEW ECONOMY SKILLS AND BLOOM'S TAXONOMY

Bloom's taxonomy classifies learning objectives into levels of complexity and specificity. Educators can use taxonomy systems like Bloom's to improve their learners' thinking. The following chart lists the types of activities that learners typically experience in Old Economy classrooms and compares them to the types of activities that are possible in New Economy classrooms, sorted by the taxonomy level of these activities. Note that the Old Economy activities listed below are most common in traditional, teacher-centered classrooms; New Economy activities are the norm in student-led academic teaming classrooms. Indeed, many of the New Economy activities listed below are *only possible* when students are able to work in teams.

Comparing Old and New Economy Classroom Activities with Bloom's Taxonomy

Level of Bloom's Taxonomy	Descriptors	Old Economy Activities	New Economy Activities
Creating	Compose Design Imagine Infer	These activities are infrequent; when they happen, there is limited student choice, students are often passive, and there is usually no intentional peer interaction or accountability.	Students search for new ways to solve problems in real-world scenarios through persistence and effort; when they use technology, it is to extend their knowledge through visionary thinking.
Evaluating	Appraise Assess Critique Judge	These activities are infrequent; when they happen, there is limited student choice, students are often passive, and there is usually no intentional peer interaction or accountability.	Students probe one another's thinking, take various positions on a subject to examine its merits, question one another's claims, provide evidence to support claims, and help others achieve goals.

Analyzing	Analyze Contrast Deduce Distinguish	These activities are infrequent; when they do happen, they are usually directed by the teacher and often follow a step-by-step directions format.	Students extend knowledge through analytical thinking and defend their analysis with evidence.
Applying	Apply Calculate Execute Practice	Students apply a skill or concept to problems selected by the teacher.	Students apply learning to new problems, have autonomy in how to solve these problems, and can defend their choices and reasoning with evidence.
Understanding	Discuss Explain Outline Summarize	The teacher teaches a skill or concept, often through lecture; technology sometimes augments the teacher's lecture. Students explain the skill or concept.	The teacher focuses on linking new learning to what students already know through mini-lessons. Students can demonstrate understanding using evidence.
Remembering	Define Label Recall Recognize	Students recall a skill or concept.	Students focus more on remembering skills than on memorizing content; they know how to use resources as reminders and can remember in context.

Sources: Anderson & Krathwohl (2001); Toth (2016). Please note: the alignment of Bloom's taxonomy to Old Economy activities and New Economy activities (right columns) was done by the authors of this book, independently of Anderson & Krathwohl.

REFERENCES

Anderson, L. W., & Krathwohl, D. R. (2001). *A taxonomy for learning, teaching, and assessing: A revision of Bloom's Taxonomy of Educational Objectives*. New York, NY: Pearson.

Association of American Colleges and Universities (AACU). (2017). *Models of global learning*. Washington, DC: Author.

Badal, S. B. (2014, January). *The business benefits of gender diversity*. Retrieved from http://news.gallup.com/businessjournal/166220/business-benefits-gender-diversity.aspx

Black, P., & Wiliam, D. (1998). Assessment and classroom learning. *Assessment in Education, 5*, 7–74.

Boekaerts, M., & Corno, L. (2005, April). Self-regulation in the classroom: A perspective on assessment and intervention. *Applied Psychology, 54*(2), 199–231.

Bouwmans, M., Runhaar, P., Wesselink, R., & Mulder, M. (2017, July). Fostering teachers' team learning: An interplay between transformational leadership and participative decision-making? *Teaching and Teacher Education, 65*, 71–80.

Brookhart, S. M., Stiggins, R. J., Wiliam, D., & McTighe, J. (2019). *Comprehensive and balanced assessment systems*. [White paper]. Retrieved from Learning Sciences International's website: https://www.dylanwiliamcenter.com/whitepapers

Capodieci, A., Rivetti, T., & Cornoldi, C. (2016, August 31). A cooperative learning classroom intervention for increasing peer's acceptance of children with ADHD. *Journal of Attention Disorders, 13*, 271–276.

CASEL. (2017). *Social and emotional learning (SEL) competencies*. Retrieved from https://casel.org/wp-content/uploads/2017/01/Competencies.pdf

Chappuis, J. (2010). *Seven strategies of assessment FOR learning*. Upper Saddle River, NJ: Pearson Education.

Claxton, G. (2007). Expanding young people's capacity to learn. *British Journal of Educational Studies, 2*(55), 115–134.

Colucci, A. (2014, February). The power of peer coaching. *Educational Horizons, 92*(3), 6–8.

Corcoran, R. P., Cheung, A., Kim, E., & Xie, C. (2018, November). Effective universal school-based social and emotional learning programs for improving academic achievement: A systematic review and meta-analysis of 50 years of research. *Educational Research Review, 25*, 56–72.

Council of Chief State School Officers. (2018). *New skills for youth*. Washington, DC: J.P. Morgan Chase.

Dandan, T., Haixue, Z., Wenfu, L., Wenjing, Y., Jiang, Q., & Qinglin, Z. (2013, September). Brain activity in using heuristic prototype to solve insightful problems. *Behavioural Brain Research, 253*, 139–144.

Des Moines Public Schools. (n.d.-a). *Data and demographics*. Retrieved from https://www.dmschools.org/academics/programs/english-language-learners/data-and-demographics/

Des Moines Public Schools (n.d.-b). *Stories and videos*. Retrieved from https://www.dmschools.org/schools-for-rigor-at-dmps/stories-and-videos/

Des Moines Public Schools. (2016, March 21). *Schools for rigor continues urban education leadership by DMPS*. Retrieved from http://www.dmschools.org/2016/03/schools-of-rigor-continues-urban-education-leadership-by-dmps/

Dweck, C. (2006). *Mindset: The new psychology of success*. New York, NY: Ballantine Books.

REFERENCES

Fastenrath, M., Coynel, D., Spalek, K., Milnik, A., Gschwind, L., Roozendaal, B., . . . de Quervain, D. J. (2014, Oct 15). Dynamic modulation of amygdala–hippocampal connectivity by emotional arousal. *Journal of Neuroscience, 34*(42), 13935–13947.

Fay, N., Garrod, S., & Carletta, J. (2000, November). Group discussion as interactive dialogue or as serial monologue: The influence of group size. (D. S. Lindsay, Ed.) *Psychological Science, 11*(6), 481–486.

Frey, D., Fisher, N., & Everlove, S. (2009). *Productive group work: How to engage students, build teamwork, and promote understanding.* Alexandria, VA: ASCD.

Galloway, R., & Lancaster, S. (n.d.). *Learning gains.* Retrieved from https://eic.rsc.org/feature /learning-gains/2000094.article

Giedd, J. N. (2012, August). The digital revolution and adolescent brain evolution. *Journal of Adolescent Health, 51*(2), 101–105.

Graham, S., Hebert, M., & Harris, K. R. (2015). Formative assessment and writing: A meta-analysis. *The Elementary School Journal, 115,* 523–547.

Granberg, C. (2016, June). Discovering and addressing errors during mathematics problem-solving—A productive struggle? *Journal of Mathematical Behavior, 42,* 33–48.

Hackman, J. R. (2004, June). *What makes for a great team?* Retrieved from http://www.apa.org /science/about/psa/2004/06/hackman.aspx

Hackman, J. R. (2011). *Collaborative intelligence: Using teams to solve hard problems.* Oakland, CA: Berrett-Koehler Publishers.

Hall, R. (n.d.). *R. Hall scripted cooperative learning research.* Retrieved from http://web.mst .edu/~rhall/cooplearning/index.html

Harvard Graduate School of Education. (2016). *How to thrive in the 21st century.* Retrieved from https://www.gse.harvard.edu/news/uk/16/11/how-thrive-21st-century

Hattie, J. (2012). *Visible learning for teachers: Maximizing impact on learning.* New York, NY: Routledge.

Hattie, J. (2015). *Hattie ranking: Backup of 195 effects related to student achievement.* Retrieved from https://visible-learning.org/hattie-ranking-backup-195-effects/

Herald, B. (2017, November 8). The case(s) against personalized learning. *Education Week, 37*(12), 4–5.

Hiebert, J., & Grouws, D. (2007). The effects of classroom mathematics teaching on students' learning. In F. K. Lester Jr. (Ed.), *Second handbook of research on mathematics teaching and learning* (pp. 371–401). Charlotte, NC: Information Age.

Hiebert, J., & Wearne, D. (2003). Developing understanding through problem solving. In R. I. Harold & L. Schoen (Eds.), *Teaching mathematics through problem solving: Grades 6–12* (pp. 3–13). Reston, VA: National Council of Teachers of Mathematics.

Hoogendoorn, S., Oosterbeek, H., & van Praag, M. (2013). The impact of gender diversity on the performance of business teams: Evidence from a field experiment. *Management Science, 59*(7), 1514–1528.

Hu, Y., Pan, Y., Shi, X., Cai, Q., Li, X., & Cheng, X. (2018, March). Inter-brain synchrony and cooperation context in interactive decision making. *Biological Psychology, 133,* 54–62.

International Society for Technology in Education (ISTE). (2018). *ISTE standards for students.* Retrieved from https://www.iste.org/standards/for-students

Jehn, K. A., Northcraft, G. B., & Neale, M. A. (1999, December). Why differences make a difference: A field study of diversity, conflict, and performance in workgroups. *Administrative Science Quarterly, 44*(4), 741–763.

Jones, S., Brush, K., Bailey, R., Brion-Meisels, G., McIntyre, J., Kahn, J. . . . Stickle, L. (2017). *Navigating SEL from the inside out.* Cambridge, MA: Harvard Graduate School of Education.

Kapur, M. (2008). Productive failure. *Cognition and Instruction, 26*(3), 379–424.

Karoly, P. (1993). Mechanisms of self-regulation: A systems view. *Annual Review Psychology, 44,* 23–52.

Kearney, E., Gebert, D., & Voelpel, S. C. (2009, June). When and how diversity benefits teams: The importance of team members' need for cognition. *The Academy of Management Journal, 52*(3), 581–596.

Keating, G. (2016). *Do you really need that meeting?* Retrieved from https://blog.intercom.com/do-you-really-need-that-meeting/

Kugler, T., Kausel, E. E., & Kocher, M. G. (2013). Are groups more rational than individuals? A review of interactive decision making in groups. *WIREs Cognitive Science, 3,* 471–482.

Lam, R. (2010). A peer review training workshop: Coaching students to give and evaluate peer feedback. *TESL Canada Journal, 27*(2), 114–127.

Leahy, S., Lyon, C., Thompson, M., & Wiliam, D. (2005). Classroom assessment: Minute-by-minute and day-by-day. *Educational Leadership, 63*(3), 18-24.

Leichtman, M. D., Camilleri, K. A., Pillemer, D. B., Amato-Wierda, C. C., Hogan, J. E., & Dongo, M. D. (2017, April). Talking after school: Parents' conversational styles and children's memory for a science lesson. *Journal of Experimental Child Psychology, 156,* 1–15.

Lleras, C. (2008). Do skills and behaviors in high school matter? The contribution of non-cognitive factors in explaining differences in educational attainment and earnings. *Social Science Research, 37,* 888–902.

Loewus, L. (2018, January 17). How much reform is too much? Teachers weigh in. *Education Week, 37*(17), 8.

MacLeod, C. M., Gopie, N., Hourihan, K. L., Neary, K. R., & Ozubko, J. D. (2010, May). The production effect: Delineation of a phenomenon. *Journal of Experimental Psychology: Learning, Memory, and Cognition,* 671–685.

Murphy, P. K., Greene, J. A., Firetto, C. M., Hendrick, B. D., Li, M., Montalbano, C., & Wei, L. (2018, April 27). Quality talk: Developing students' discourse to promote high-level comprehension. *American Education Research Journal, 55*(5), 113–1160.

National Education Association. (2018). *Partnership for 21st century learning.* Washington, DC: Author.

Newmann, F. M., Wehlage, G. G., & Lamborn, S. D. (1992). The significance and sources of student achievement. In F. M Newmann (Ed.), *Student engagement and achievement in American secondary schools.* New York, NY: Teachers College Press.

Organization for Economic Cooperation and Development (OECD). (2017). *PISA 2015 assessment and analytical framework: Science, reading, mathematic, financial literacy and collaborative problem solving.* Paris, France: Author.

Organization for Economic Cooperation and Development (OECD). (2018). *The future of education and skills: Education 2030.* Paris, France: Author.

Penczynski, S. P. (2016, October). Persuasion: An experimental study of team decision making. *Journal of Economic Psychology, 56,* 244–261.

Portnow, S., Downer, J. T., & Brown, J. (2018, June). Reductions in aggressive behavior within the context of a universal, social emotional learning program: Classroom- and student-level mechanisms. *Journal of School Psychology, 68,* 38–52.

Revington, S. (n.d.). *Defining authentic learning.* Retrieved from http://authenticlearning.weebly.com/

Roberge, M.-E., & van Dick, R. (2010, December). Recognizing the benefits of diversity: When and how does diversity increase group performance? *Human Resource Management Review, 20*(4), 295–308.

Schacter, J. (2000). Does individual tutoring produce optimal learning? *American Educational Research Journal, 37*(3), 801–829.

Simmons, J. (2003, May). Responders are taught, not born. *Journal of Adolescent & Adult Literacy, 46*(8), 684–693.

Sousa, D. A. (2016). *Engaging the rewired brain.* West Palm Beach, FL: Learning Sciences International.

Stahl, G. K., Maznevski, M. L., Voigt, A., & Jonsen, K. (2009, November). Unraveling the effects of cultural diversity in teams: A meta-analysis of research on multicultural work groups. *Journal of International Business Studies,* 1–20.

Stanford Center for Opportunity Policy in Education. (2014, January 28). *Student-centered learning approaches are effective in closing the opportunity gap.* Retrieved from https://edpolicy.stanford.edu/news/articles/1137

REFERENCES

Stein, M. K., Smith, M. S., Henningsen, M. A., & Silver, E. A. (2009). *Implementing standards-based mathematics instruction: A casebook for professional development.* New York, NY: Teachers College Press.

Stiggins, R. J., Arter, J. A., Chappuis, J., & Chappuis, S. (2004). *Classroom assessment for student learning: Doing it right—using it well.* Portland, OR: ETS Assessment Training Institute.

Stipek, D. (1996). Motivation and instruction. In D. Berliner & R. Calfee (Eds.), *Handbook of educational psychology.* New York, NY: Macmillan.

Sturgis, C., & Casey, K. (2018). *Designing for equity: Leveraging competency-based education to ensure all students succeed.* Vienna, VA: iNACOL. https://creativecommons.org/licenses /by/4.0/

Szymanski, C., Pesquita, A., Brennan, A. A., Perdikis, D., Enns, J. T., Brick, T. R., . . . Lindenberger, U. (2017, May 15). Teams on the same wavelength perform better: Inter-brain phase synchronization constitutes a neural substrate for social facilitation. *NeuroImage,* 425–436.

Tadich, B., Deed, C., Campbell, C., & Prain, V. (2007). Student engagement in the middle years: A year 8 case study. *Issues in Educational Research, 17*(2), 256–271.

Taylor, R. D., Oberle, E., Durlak, J. A., & Weissberg, R. P. (2017, July/August). Promoting positive youth development through school-based social and emotional learning interventions: A meta-analysis of follow-up effects. *Child Development, 88*(4), 1156–1171.

Toth, M. D. (2016). *Who moved my standards? Joyful teaching in an age of change: A SOAR-ing tale.* West Palm Beach, FL: Learning Sciences International.

Trisolini, D. C., Petilli, M. A., & Daini, R. (2018, January 1). Is action video gaming related to sustained attention of adolescents? *Quarterly Journal of Experimental Psychology, 71*(5), 1033–1039.

Van den Bossche, P., Gijselaers, W., Segers, M., & Kirschner, P. (2006, October). Social and cognitive factors driving teamwork in collaborative learning environments. *Small Group Research, 37*(5), 490–521.

Vangrieken, K., Boon, A., Dochy, F., & Kyndt, E. (2017). Group, team, or something in between? Conceptualizing and measuring team entitativity. *Frontline Learning Research, 5*(4), 1–41.

Vartanian, O., Beatty, E. L., Smith, I., Blackler, K., Lam, Q., & Forbes, S. (2018, September). One-way traffic: The inferior frontal gyrus controls brain activation in the middle temporal gyrus and inferior parietal lobule during divergent thinking. *Neuropsychologia, 118,* 68-78.

Wang, T., Ren, X., & Schweizer, K. (2017, March–April). Learning and retrieval processes predict fluid intelligence over and above working memory. *Intelligence, 61,* 29–36.

Wiemers, E. A., & Redick, T. S. (2018, January). Working memory capacity and intra-individual variability of proactive control. *Acta Psychologica, 182,* 21–31.

Wiliam, D., & Leahy, S. (2015). *Embedding formative assessment: Practical techniques for K–12 classrooms.* West Palm Beach, FL: Learning Sciences International.

World Economic Forum. (2015). *New vision for education: Unlocking the potential of technology* (Rep.). Retrieved from http://www3.weforum.org/docs/WEFUSA_NewVisionforEducation _Report2015.pdf

Zimmerman, B. J., & Schunk, D. H. (2011). Self-regulated learning and performance. In B. J. Zimmerman & D. H. Schunk (Eds.), *Handbook of self-regulated learning and performance* (pp. 1–12). New York, NY: Routledge.